D1766521

CONTENTS

PART 1: THE UNITY OF KNOWLEDGE
THESIS

LIMERICK LIBRARIES

3 0027 00820375 1

UNITY OF

KNOWLEDGE

A Whole System Approach To The Coherence Theory of
Truth.

Yemi Adex Adeniran PhD

© 2016 by Yemi Adex Adeniran
All rights reserved.

No part of this book may be reproduced
in any form by any electronic or mechanical means
(including photocopying, recording, and
information storage and retrieval) without permission in
writing from the publisher.

The Unity of Knowledge: A whole System Approach
To The Coherence Theory Of Truth, published by Yemi Adex Adeniran PhD
includes bibliograhical references and index.

ISBN - 978-1-5262-0225-3

215

PART 1: THE UNITY OF KNOWLEDGE THESIS

INTRODUCTION TO THE UNITY OF KNOWLEDGE THESIS

THE SYNERGISTIC LOGIC OF THE UNITY OF KNOWLEDGE

Fragmented sub-systems of knowledge are inadvertently created in the ongoing war between the proponents of scientific system of knowledge and religious system of knowledge.

This war needs to end.

To end this war, there is a need to redirect the fruitless energies that both camps are currently exuding in fighting tough to defend their claims to knowledge.

I'm advocating in this book for a more fruitful 'one system of knowledge'.

I interact and critique the methodological naturalistic approach to knowledge and the dogmatic, closed religious system approach to knowledge and then suggest the synergistic approach to the unity of knowledge.

The book is written to engage both the academics and the general public in the current debate regarding science / religion divide. It is therefore a lucid analysis of what I referred to as the 'false bifurcation between science knowledge and religion knowledge'. This is a wake up call to the extremists on both sides of the divide - the 'scientismists' (the proponents of scientism) and the proponents of the dogmatic, closed religious system approach to knowledge.

It contains academic references and quotes of interviews and views expressed in blogs and so on, in order to critique arguments put forward by both sides, thereby steering the debate towards the book's unity of knowledge thesis that ensures a whole system approach to the coherence theory of truth.

Chapter 1

THE SYNERGY OF KNOWLEDGE

The Whole Is Greater Than the Sum of Its Parts

The Shortcoming of the methodological, naturalistic approach to knowledge is engraved in scientism – a religious and scientific outlook to life – it is the view that science explains everything important. The advocacy for my thesis of one system of knowledge needs to clear one hurdle, 'scientism'. This is an important obstacle that needs to be removed. Scientism is undoubtedly a barrier to the construct of 'one system of knowledge.' Burkeman [1] is right to describe Sam Harris, one of the four new atheistic horsemen as one 'elephant in the room,' 'of one system of truth,' I hasten to add. I couldn't agree more with Burkeman when he asks 'Is science overstepping its bounds? He answers in the affirmative, clearly yes.

The clog in the wheel of progress, as it were, to one system of knowledge is scientism. Pinker's blind defence of scientism in his article, 'Science Is not your Enemy [2]' represents such a clog.

Pinker in his lopsided view in favour of scientism, assumes that, the Age of Reason's stalwarts, mostly are ardent scientists but he fails to mention that most of them are theists too. Galileo, Kepler, Isaac Newton, Rene Descarte, Charles Babbage, the father of computing, James Clarke Maxwell and so on, and in fact, the scientific enterprise has deep theological root, for example, the science of Isaac Newton, or that some of them were at least deistic' in their conception of modern scientific development, for example Gottfried Leibniz, John Locke and so on.

While scientism's contemporary most zealous proponents

---

[1] 'Scientism' wars: 'there's an elephant in the room, and its name is Sam Harris'.Oliver Burkeman's Blog in the guardian of 27 Aug13 '

[2] Steven Pinker, 'Science Is not your Enemy - An impassioned plea to neglected novelists, and embattled professors and tenure-less historians.' The New Republic August 6 2013.

include the late Christopher Hitchen, Richard Dawkins, Sam Harris and Steven Pinker, even the most agnostic naturalist about religion, Michael Ruse is not immune from its addictive impact. Ruse, [3] an agnostic atheist has rationalised along the line of common objection, that science is not compatible with religion given the repeatability nature of science that makes it universal, whereas, the religious people instead have polarised views. That is, the Muslims, the protestants, the Catholics and Mormons have completely set of religious worldviews.

I would argue that Ruse's view here, does not hold water. In fact Ruse misses the point. No one expects religion, a subjective phenomenon to be scientific, but because religious people hold polarised views doesn't in any way preclude them from being scientific. I would rather argue that both science and religion, according to my thesis here, have roots in one system of knowledge.

On the relationship between science and religion, Ruse's scale on which of the two is more important, tips more in favour of science than religion. He said:

Christianity cannot simply ignore the rules and norms of science especially the standards of reasoned arguments……..as with the application of law theory, great care must be taken to see that theological conclusions are infused with the findings of really up-to-date science. As the science changes so may this conclusion. [4]

Ruse's view here, is typical of the confusion that arises from doing science on the naturalistic or materialistic paradigm. This paradigm assumes that Christianity in rejecting the reductionist

---

[3] Keith Ward vs Michael Ruse on Mind, Consciousness & The God Question - Unbelievable? // 2013-09-28 Unbelievable? Radio SaturdayPremierChristianRadio.www.premierradio.org.uk/shows/sat urday/unbelievable.aspx (accessed June 22, 2013).

[4] Michael Ruse, Science and Spirituality – Making room for faith in the age of science, Cambridge University Press; 1 edition (March 8, 2010), 235

claim of supremacy of science over religion is ignoring the rules and norms of science. Far from it, the Christian theistic view is that doing modern science is made possible in the first place, on the Christian theistic paradigm, for example, the Newtonian science originated within the Christian Western culture, in comparison with the impracticalities of doing science within the atheistic Marxist paradigm in China. [5]

On miracles, Ruse being Humean in outlook philosophically, claims that

'…naturally, water does not simply turn into wine. To claim otherwise is to violate the norms of science. Hence one must argue that if religion insists this must be true, then it is encroaching illegitimately on the realm of science'. [6]

The underline thinking behind Ruse's assertion here, is that Christianity by affirming the possibility of the miraculous, is 'encroaching illegitimately on the realm of science'. Nothing could be farther from the truth. The laws of nature exhibit themselves in regularities. In Newtonian science, regularities manifest, as bodies attract with gravitational force relative to their masses and distance. Under Boyles' law of gasses, regularities exhibit predictable behaviour, for example, volume of gasses decrease in a confined space, howbeit, when frozen water expands. Likewise, flammable substance, for example, petrol ignites when it is exposed to flame.

Hence, the occurrence of miracle, is God intervening in the regularities of the laws of nature that he has created – God turning the regularities on their heads as it were. It is plausible to assert on

---

[5] John Lennox, 'God is Irrelevant': Discussion John Lennox (Official Recording) Faith And Global Engagement Hong Kong University. Lennox, here, alluded to Needham's conclusion on cultural context which made modern science feasible. Lennox commented on Joseph Needham's science and civilization in China thus: 'lack of rise of modern science in China is due to the fact that Chinese thinking lacks central idea of a monotheistic – one God as the creator who created the universe according to rational laws.'

[6] Ruse, 235.

---

the Christian conviction model of reality, that, if God created the laws of nature in the first place, he is not bound by them. God has moral right to tinker with the laws to serve his purposes, if you like. For that's how it seems to the human reasoning.

As John Foster puts it thus:

"...the only way of making sense of the notion of a law of nature ...is by construing a law as the causing of the associated regularity, and the only remotely plausible account of such causing would be in terms of the agency of God." So, by which ever route, we are led to the conclusion that the regularities are brought about by God. [7]

DOES SCIENTIFIC PROGRESS POSE A THREAT TO RELIGIOUS BELIEFS?

So, while in Newtonian science, God is in charge of the laws of nature, in Peter 'Atkinsian science, science is god, the alpha and omega of the atheistic universe. He was interviewed about his book 'On Being' on BBC Radio 4. In answering the question "why are we here?" and others, Atkins said:

'it's just by accident, we just stumble into being.'

'Science, has all the evidence it needs that the universe is "entirely without purpose'

'You are born an intelligent animal with no soul or spirit and there is "I think that science exposes the wonder of the world as it is. You don't need fantasies to build that sense of wonder. Science is true nothing left alive after the body has died.'

"I think that science exposes the wonder of the world as it is. You don't need fantasies to build that sense of wonder. Science is true

---

[7] John Foster, "Regularities, Laws of nature and the Existence of God". Proceedings of the Aristotelian Society, New Series, Vol. 101, (2001), pp. 145-161 Published by: The Aristotelian Society.

Article Stable URL: http://www.jstor.org/stable,4545343 (accessed 12 August, 2013).1

glory, whereas religion is fabricated glory."' [8]

Simple logic is all that it takes to refute rather than rebut the philosophy underpinning Atkins' claims in favour of scientism in the above quotes. Atkins' claim, that, we're here by accident, that we simply stumble into existence, itself, presupposes a chain of causal events from how the universe came into existence to how man came into existence, which in Atkins' view, are merely physical events.

But one can argue that an accident as a phenomenon occurs in tandem with other probable causal event(s). An accident doesn't just occur unless it is triggered by something. If, in Atkins' outlook to life, man's existence materialised just by accident, I hasten to add, something must have triggered man's existence. There is no getting away from this raison d'être.

As an eminent philosopher, Midgley who debated Professor Atkins on the same BBC Radio 4's Today Programme put it thus,

"An accident only makes sense within a whole….."

The foregoing goes to depict how scientism blurs the picture of reality of the one system of knowledge / truth that exists. We need to therefore, get past the myopic views that underlie scientism, to a broad-mindedness that the one system of truth engenders.

Conversely, the religious system approach to knowledge / Truth becomes equally problematic to my thesis of the whole 'one system of knowledge' by those who dogmatically oppose scientific findings based on their interpretation of a few bible passages for which an alternative biblical interpretation exists. I wish to differentiate here between taking a theistic stance for the essentials with regards to Christian truth claims and the inessentials that do not diminish in any respect the theistic fundamental Christian truth claims. The wise rule of course, for truth abiding theistic believer is 'no compromise on essentials fundamental teaching of the bible, but to give the benefit

---

[8]Quoted in "Does science have all the answers? By Tom Colls BBC Radio 4 Today programme Page last updated at 08:51 GMT, Thursady, 17 ,March 2011 http://news.bbc.co.uk/today/hi/today/newsid_9410000/9410486.stm. Internet accessed on 4th October 2013.

of the doubt to the inessential views.

Such inessential viewpoints (in the sense that holding them does not have any negative impact on the biblical faith of the Christian scientist) to my mind, include opposing viewpoints on scientific evidence regarding the age of the earth /universe, as they are often expressed in the old earth / young earth debate.

THE GEOLOGICAL EVIDENTIAL SPLIT

The argument, as to whether the rock and fossil record is either evidence of catastrophic event, for example, the flood occurrence of Noah's days or evolutionary occurrence hinges mainly, on the dating system that is used. The evolutionary scientists often favour the use of radiometric dating system to measure the age of the rock to justify their claim of ancient or old earth having an age that implies several billions of years. It is a mistaken belief to assume that only atheistic or theistic evolutionists belong in the ancient or old earth camp. In actual fact, many Christian scientists (who are not evolutionists) are ancient or old earth advocates too.

One faction of the young earth scientists argues for an evidence for a young earth using the process of radioactive carbon dating. This is the method in which the activity of radioactive carbon (carbon-14) present in bones, wood, or ash found in archaeological sites, is measured. Since the rate at which this radioactive carbon (carbon-14) decreases in time is known, the approximate age of fossilised wood or coal can be determined by comparing it to carbon-14 activity in presently living organic matter. Since carbon 14 only measures in thousands of years not exceed 100,000 years, the young earth scientists claim that the age of the earth is far less than a hundred thousand years to rebut the old earth scientists' claim of the age of the earth estimated to be about sixty billion years.

THE POLARISED VIEWS AMONGST CHRISTIAN THEISTIC SCHOLARS

How the seven days of the book of Genesis are viewed differ as to whether a Christian scientist is from a young or old earth school of thought. There is a consensus amongst young earth and old earth Christian scientists that the first six days of Genesis are six creation days, and that on the seventh day God rested from his work. But this is where the similarity between the young and old earth scientists ends. They part company as to whether the first six days are literal days of 24 hours period. That is a Calendar day view of six consecutive days of creation in the book of Genesis. This is the young earth scientist position. The young earth scientists do argue that Yom the Hebrew word meaning day in Genesis 1 is associated with numerals 1-6 days followed by the phrase "and evening and morning." Likewise in I Samuel 17:6 Yom (day) is followed by numerals implying that evening and morning constitutes one calendar day:

"For forty days the Philistine came forward every morning and evening and took his stand."

So, here, Goliath came precisely for 40 Calendar days. The days here may well be 40 consecutive days but does this mean that the six days of creation in Genesis 1 can't be interpreted differently to imply day ages, as in fact, the Christian Old earth scientists have done? The old earth scientists do argue that while the Hebrew word Yom (day) in the Old Testament does in some instances imply a calendar day, it also in other instances, in the bible, connotes a longer period of time beyond 24 hours period. Thus in Hosea 6:2

'After two days he will revive us; on the third day he will restore us, that we may live in his presence.'

Though a number precedes the word Yom in Hosea 6:2, this, is not a reference to a 24 hours period. The old earth scientists argued that, the position of many biblical and Hebrew scholars, is that Yom (day) in six days of creation in Genesis can be interpreted to mean a very long period of time. For example, the sixth day in which God created Adam who engaged in tending the garden, naming all the animals and becoming a husband to Eve after he must have been lonely for a while, must be interpreted to be longer than a twenty four hours period.

LITERAL INTERPRETATIONAL VIEW OF TRUTH

It's important to qualify the use of the word 'literal' here. There is more than one form of literal interpretation of the days of creation found in the book of Genesis.

One form of literal interpretation of the days of creation of Genesis, is taking the meaning of the days on their face value, hence the form of literal interpretation assumed by the young earth scientists being consecutive days of twenty four hours period. The young earth scientist's view of truth is based only on their form of literal interpretation of the days of creation found in the book of Genesis 1.

The other form of literal interpretation of days of Genesis, takes a more generous approach to presuppose that each day of creation represents not a 24 hours period but rather a long period of time. This is the Christian Old earth scientist position.

In this regard, the old earth scientists' form of literal interpretation of the days of creation in the book of Genesis correlates with the expression 'in the day' of Genesis 2:4. So the old earth scientists interpret the days of creation as day ages, that is an era rather than six consecutive days of 24 hours period.

The commonality here, is that, both forms of interpretation being Christian and conservative in outlook, assume a literal interpretation that depicts the genuineness, the earnestness with which both opposing camps take the bible as a divine literature that it is. There is no question that both camps take the Bible as the sole authoritative word of the Personal infinite God who has spoken to finite man through propositional revelation.

Both camps concur that man was created by God, also that the human race descended from Adam and Eve unlike the theistic evolutionist's position that life came by evolutionary processes. They both agreed that the appearance of man on earth is more recent, that is, just thousands of years and not millions of years. It is also important to note that both young earth and Christian old earth scientists' positions are far removed (in terms of their fundamental position grounded in the biblical truth claims) from the view of theistic evolutionists.

This area of commonality amongst both young and Christian Old earth scientists is consistent with my CT Conviction model (see Part 11 of this book). In my view, this is what I regard as the essentials or Christian theistic core beliefs with which no compromise can be entertained. Therefore other issues as to whether creation days are

six consecutive (Calendar) days or day ages, are for the purposes of this book of unity of knowledge, the inessentials.
These inessentials cannot be allowed to stand in the way of the unity of science knowledge / (Christian) religion knowledge.

Within the CT conviction model, the notion of divine communication presupposes the existence of propositional revelation in which the Personal Infinite God has spoken to the finite man. Divine communication here connotes how God has communicated knowledge to man. This wholesome knowledge, since the Enlightenment has been bifurcated into science knowledge / religion knowledge which as I have argued in Part 11 of this book is an unhealthy false bifurcation of knowledge.

Chapter 2

ONE SYSTEM OF KNOWLEDGE

Having argumentatively cleared the hurdle of 'scientism' out of the way of advocacy for the one system of knowledge and having depolarized the views amongst young earth and Christian old earth scientists with regards to among others, the age of the earth, the opposing interpretative frameworks on the days of Genesis and so on, we can now focus on what the source of 'one system of knowledge' is, from the Christian theistic worldview.

To pursue this line of thought we need to further elucidate the CT Conviction model's divine communication processes namely, general revelation versus special revelation (see Part 11 chapter 10 for introduction to this.) The implication here is that the 'one system of knowledge' entails special revelation (the propositional revelation) and general revelation. The general revelation is the non-propositional revelation that accounts for God's act in the natural world. The rational argumentation by Francis Schaeffer, that through propositional revelation, propositional truth, regarding man's knowledge of science and also biblical historical account were communicated to man, by the Personal Infinite God, is instructive here. How? The oldest of the doctrinal standards of the Reformed churches, Belgic Confession (1561), article 2,- stated:

Article 2 - How God makes Himself known to us

We know Him by two means: First, by the creation, preservation, and government of the universe; which is before our eyes as a most beautiful book, wherein all creatures, great and small, are as so many letters leading us to perceive clearly the invisible qualities of God namely His eternal power and deity, as the apostle Paul says in Rom 1:20. All these things are sufficient to convict men and leave them without excuse. Second, He makes Himself more clearly and fully known to us by His holy and divine Word as far as is necessary for us in this life, to His glory and our salvation. [9]

This goes to show that the reformed Christian stance supports the

---

[9] THE CONFESSION OF FAITH or The Belgic Confession
www.upcsa.org.za/docs-docs/belgic_confession.pdf

thesis of 'one system of knowledge' herein advocated.

A WHOLE SYSTEM APPROACH TO THE COHERENCE THEORY OF TRUTH

The coherence theory of truth posits that the truth of any proposition or belief consists in its coherence with a set of propositions or beliefs. Here I'm proposing a whole system approach to the coherence theory of truth. The implication being that truth becomes a property of the whole system of propositions or beliefs. That is a proposition or belief is only true to the extent to which it coheres with other set of propositions or beliefs within the whole system of truth.

In line with my thesis of the one system of knowledge therefore, the atheistic assumption of scientism, that science is all real knowledge there is, which in turn presupposes that the only reality is the natural world, is incoherent in light of the above definition of the coherence theory of truth. We all of course know that the natural world is about what is empirical, that is knowledge derived from experience of the senses. Science is the study of nature but natural science is limited to the nomological explanation of the scientific investigation which entails repeatability or reproducible description of nature as in testable scientific experiments under controlled conditions, or scientific observation done in astronomical space exploration, for example, by NAZA. Hence science has as its goal, the description, explanation, prediction and control of the natural world.

What the foregoing analysis depicts is the difference between science and scientism. We've seen that the feature of science consists in repeatability or reproducibility or empiricism. Scientism therefore is merely a philosophical construct, a dogmatic worldview about scientific knowledge in so far as it projects science as a sole means of knowledge. In doing so, this worldview, the religious belief of the 'scientismists' (the proponents of scientism), is incoherent with a set of other propositions or beliefs within the whole system of truth or reality. For example, within the whole system of knowledge / truth or reality, the aggregate propositions or beliefs include the Judeo-Christian worldview, which posits the existence of knowledge beyond the natural world or natural science.

More specifically as my thesis here depicts, there is one system of truth leading to one source of knowledge of the natural world or natural science and the transcendental or metaphysical realm.

To represent my critique of the incoherence of atheistic scientism with regards to its claim that science is the real knowledge there is, let's argue this philosophically thus:

1. Science has astronomically revolutionised our world in ways that are undoubtedly beneficial to mankind through advancement in science and technology.

2. There is no other source of real knowledge, and certainly, no other form of knowledge can achieve these feats in a demonstrably empirical way as science does, in that it amazes us this much.

3. Therefore, science is the only real knowledge there is.

Since the coherence theory of truth posits that the truth of any proposition or belief consists in its coherence with a set of propositions or beliefs, I hasten to add, as I claim in my thesis, within the whole system of knowledge / truth, the first two premises are inconsistent with each other. The second premise is false, the argument is therefore invalid as the conclusion does not follow the premises.

To represent my critique of the incoherence of atheistic scientism with regards to its claim that the only reality is the natural world, let's argue this philosophically thus:

1. Unlike scientific propositions that are derivable from the natural world, we have no way to empirically falsify religious metaphysical or ontological propositions such as 'God necessarily exists'.

2. Naturalistic explanations evidentially are falsifiable and so have the most credible explanatory power of reality.

3. Therefore, the perfect reality is the natural world.

The above philosophical argument represents the perfect presumption of atheistic scientism with regard to the natural world being the perfect reality. The audacious claim here, is myopic, in its non- inclusiveness of reality beyond the natural world. The second premise is false as the natural world is only a fragment of the ultimate reality. Therefore the argument is invalid as the conclusion does not follow the premises. The proposition that the perfect reality is the natural world is incoherent as it does not cohere with other propositions within the whole system of knowledge / truth, namely that the transcendence or the metaphysical realm is a reality. Hence the natural world is only a fragment of the ultimate reality.

To represent my critique of the incoherence of atheistic scientism with regards to its claim to the ultimate truth in contradistinction to the real domain of the ultimate truth, let's argue this philosophically thus:

1. As the goal of science is the description, explanation, prediction and control of the natural world, it is a search for 'reliable knowledge.'

2. Scientific 'reliable knowledge' does not equate the ultimate truth.

3. The search for the ultimate truth lies outside the nomological explanation that underpins the scientific investigation of the natural world.

4. The search for the ultimate truth lies within the axiological explanation that underpins the realm beyond the natural world.

5. Hence, science is not a search for truth but a search for 'reliable knowledge.'

6.Therefore, the search for the ultimate truth lies within the domain of transcendence or metaphysical realm of the absolute truth.

The validity of the philosophical argument above is apparent from its logical premises1-5 leading to the conclusion, that, why the search for the ultimate truth lies outside the scientific investigation of the natural world (a subset of reality), it belongs in the domain of transcendence or metaphysical realm (the ultimate reality) of the absolute truth.

The philosophy that is implied here of course, is, the theistic conception of transcendence. There are other two conceptions of transcendence in the Western philosophical system, namely, Platonism (Plato's reality of forms) and Kantian's world of Noumena.

There is a consensus amongst these three conceptions of transcendence as Munitz (1990) puts it thus:

"They unite in the claim that the domain of space-time, entities and phenomena does not exhaust reality." [10]

It is a matter of fact that science has profound historical Christian root that finds expression in the biblical scripture including Hebrew 1:3:

The Son is the radiance of God's glory...sustaining all things by His powerful word"

The fundamental principles underpinning the development of modern science originate from the Judeo-Christian worldview. So the scientists who were touch bearers of the quest for modern scientific knowledge are theists. For example, it is telling that the following scientists held metaphysical assumptions without which doing modern science is impossible. Their worldviews presuppose there being regularities, uniformity, rationality, intelligibility and conditions that are conducive for doing modern science.

Johannes Kepler (1571-1630) in doing science felt, quote "I was thinking God's thought after him."

That the founders of the royal society were influenced by their Judeo Christian worldview is evident in their metaphysical reflections, for example, Robert Boyles (1627-1691) wrote a book title "The wisdom of God Manifested in Works of Creation." Isaac Newton

---

[10] Milton K Munitz. Cosmic Understanding: Philosophy and Science of the Universe. Princeton University Press, 1990. P.186

(1642-1727)- affirms that:

"This most beautiful system of the sun, planets and comets could only proceed from the counsel and dominion of an intelligent being."

John Polkinhorne, the Cambridge scientist's brute facts analysis is instructive in understanding the principle underpinning an aspect of my thesis of one system of knowledge / truth, namely that the relationship between science and religion is not 'Either Or' but Both And' endeavour. Polkinghorne [11] puts it thus:

"If we are to understand the nature of reality, we have only two possible starting points: etheir the brute fact of the physical world or the brute fact of a divine will and purpose behind that physical world."

The 'brute facts' are compelling starting points. One starting point is for the naturalist, 'the brute fact of the physical world'. The other is for the theist, 'the brute fact of a divine will and purpose behind that physical world'.

Isn't it obvious in light of the philosophical argument above that the naturalistic presupposition which the naturalist adopts as the starting point for exploring the nature of reality only leads the naturalist to an end - a limited discovery, a fraction of reality, the reliable knowledge of the natural world period and nothing more. This spells the end of the road of discovery of reality for the naturalist. The materialistic or reductionistic paradigm that the naturalist employs here is, deficient, as it is incoherent for exploring the ultimate reality and cannot answer the most important questions in life. For example, there is no way to first scientifically prove that the person one intends to marry loves one, in order to make the right decision as to whether-or not to enter into a lifelong marriage relationship with him / her.

The theistic starting point on the other hand is presupposed by the 'brute fact of a divine will and purpose behind that physical world'.

The theistic perspective is designed to answer the most important

---

[11] John Polkinghorne, Serious Talk: Science and Religion in Dialogue. (1995)

big questions in life. The 'brute fact of divine will' as a starting point posits God who knows the end from the beginning. The theistic proposition for exploring reality, in light of my thesis of one whole system of knowledge / truth or reality, presupposes that the search for truth lies outside the scientific investigation of the natural world (a subset of reality). I have by rational argumentation depicted that the search for truth or proposition for understanding the nature of reality that Polkinghorne alluded to, belongs in the domain of transcendence or metaphysical realm (the ultimate reality) of the absolute truth.

A pivotal point that this work intends to drive home, is that, with different aspects of reality, in the main, science and religion turned into warring parts by players in the academy, we will never reach and reap from the wholesome reality that is only open to us, by pursuit of one system of knowledge.

As the central theme of the poem that inspired the late Brown University professor's book aptly and poetically put it thus:

"Things fall apart; the centre cannot hold....." [12]

THE PERSPECTIVES ON THE ASPECTS OF REALITY

There are different perspectives on the aspects of reality in the academy. To Stephen Hawking the ultimate questions of life regarding the purpose for man's existence, the reason there is something rather than nothing, include, how can we understand the world in which we find ourselves? What is the nature of reality? Did the universe need a creator? - and so on are best answered by science. This is that scientism rearing its arrogant head again! How do we know this? We know because he claimed that science can operate beyond its remit of repeatability or reproducibility:

"Scientists have become the bearers of the torch of discovery in our quest for knowledge." [13]

In this vein, atheistic scientists always tell us that one day science

---

[12] Chinua Achebe, Things Fall Apart. William Heinemann Ltd UK 1958.
[13] Stephen Hawking, Leonard, Mlodinow. The Grand Design New Answers To The Ultimate Question Of Life, published by Bantam Books in 2010. P.1

will explain everything. This view represents the position of Richard Dawkins and other celebrated atheists.

The late Sir Peter Medawar of the Cambridge university who was awarded the Nobel Prize for medicine, however parted company with "scientismists" on 'science will explain everything mentality' including the existential questions of origin of life , the universe and purpose for existence, when he wrote, to, on one hand, eulogise science for its place, as the greatest human endeavour, as we would all also concur, but in the same breath set the record straight, to emphasise the foolhardiness of setting unrealistic expectation for science:

"Science is a great and glorious enterprise, the most successful, I argue, that human beings have ever engaged in. To reproach it for its inability to answer all the questions we should like to put to it is no more sensible than to reproach a railway locomotive for not flying or, in general, not performing the operation for which it was not designed." [14]

Sir Peter Medawar, therefore left no stone unturned in his unequivocal conclusion that, it is the magesterium, which is the domain of teaching authority of religion that has the explanatory power to answer the big questions of life.

"It is not to science, therefore but to metaphysics, imaginative literature or religion that we must turn for answers to questions having to do with first and last things." [15]

---

[14] Peter Medawar, 'The limit of Science' (Oxford University Press (1987)

[15] Medawar,

Chapter 3

LAYERS OF THE EXPLANATION OF THE ULTIMATE REALITY

There are different layers of explanation of the ultimate reality. There are two categories of explanation. Let's call these categories, the model of levels of explanation of reality including mechanism / agency level of explanation of reality and mechanism / meaning level of explanation of reality.

In the first category of explanation, the model of mechanism / agency level of explanation of reality, agency implies the intelligence for construing or interpreting the explanation of the ultimate reality at the most deeper level. Mechanism on the contrary originates from universal mechanism that is closely related to materialism and reductionism. This is the philosophy that the universe is reducible to completely mechanical level of motion and matter. This explains why most contemporary atheistic scientists also assume a deterministic explanatory framework, that all phenomena can be explained mechanistically, in terms of natural laws that govern motion and matter.

We need to consider the nature of explanation in order to further explore different levels of explanation of reality. Philosophers offer us a means of exploring more abstractly, different levels of reality and arguably we all are philosophers. There is hardly a discipline in the academy that doesn't operate within a philosophy. We have philosophy of science, philosophy of religion and so on. Theology in fact, once being the queen of the sciences.

So philosophically, there are different levels of reality. There is the level of medium size objects which include physical objects on our planet, man (that is, his or her physical constituent. Man is more than matter, I hasten to add.), chairs, tables, other planets etc. There is an upper level of quantum reality. This is the level of a very small unit of matter that particles of an atom consist of, called quarks. Illustratively, the new frontier of nanotechnology where measurements occur at nanometres (nm) is instructive here.

We're all familiar with technology at micro level with our PCs, iPhones, iPads and so on. Scientists are now experimenting with building machines at nanoscales, for example nano cars in molecular chemistry. A micrometer is one millionth of a metre, but that is huge compared to units of measurement on a nanoscale, where a nanometre (mn) is one billionth of a metre. But a nanometre (mn) is still large compared to the atomic scale. An atom is 0.1 mn. This is an incredible world of the smallest atomic substances, the level of quantum reality.

On the level above quantum physics is the realm of electrons and atoms. There is a level of chemical reality consisting of chemicals and its associated bonds. There is also the anatomic realm, the level of biology where our bodies are composed of millions of cells, the nature's nano machines.

Then there are the higher levels (I include here the spiritual realm) of the metaphysical realm including minds, numbers, angels and God.

We've analysed the levels of reality at great length of specific details in order to uncover the drivers for the worldviews held by the people who either study or work with the objects, properties and so on, of different levels of reality. For all the levels of reality that fall within the magesterium or domain of natural science on this planet, other planets, quantum reality and quantum physics, given the advancement in science and technology since the enlightenment, it is understandable that, majority of the scientists involved in the study of these levels of reality are reductionistic in their explanation of reality. The snag is, this level of explanation is limited as its explanatory power reduces reality to scientific methods of physics and chemistry. So a methodological reductionist explains these levels of reality scientifically in terms of physics and chemistry involved.

Bertrand Russell (1872-1970) sums up this worldview thus:

"What science cannot discover, mankind cannot know."

Really?

According to the New Scientist's article entitled, "That's Life" 2005, an adult human being, a typical adult male or female's body, apart from water, consists of elements including about 67%

oxygen, 20% carbon, 10%, hydrogen and 3% Nitrogen. So we may ask, is man made only of his or her human molecular formula? The answer you get to this sort of question from scientists operating from the methodological reductionistic sphere, is in the affirmative, yes.

However, to follow this line of reasoning through, let's suppose we have a scenario in which an eligible bachelor Romeo meets Juliet and the two lovers fall headlong in love. One day Juliet asks Romeo how much of her, he, Romeo really knows. Romeo, a passionate scientist tries to really impress Juliet of his knowledge of human molecular formula and says to her: I know for sure who you are: As a female, you are composed of less water than I am a male. Also you are about 67% oxygen, 20% carbon, 10%, hydrogen and 3% Nitrogen. Anyone who has ever fallen in love knows that this kind of mechanical answer, in the least, is anything romantic, and certainly not the answer that the love struck Juliet expects from her Romeo. There is certainly more to a human being, at the level of meaning that has a better explanatory power. Hence we can logically conclude that man is more than the description of his or her molecular formula.

This lop-sided view of reality however creates a vacuum in the whole system of the ultimate reality. To bridge the gap that exists in the whole system of the ultimate reality, we need to seek the irreducible explanatory power of the higher level of reality, namely the transcendent. Again Munitz's description of the conception of the transcendent from the theistic perspective is instructive here:

" For the theist, the transcendent is identified with God, the Supreme Being, who is wholly different from the spatio- temporal world of objects that He created." [16]

This form of explanation is ontological in nature. It is the agency level of explanation of reality. This involves intelligence for construing or interpreting the explanation of the ultimate reality at the most deeper level. We shall further explore the conception of the transcendence below. Within the second category of explanation, the model of mechanism / meaning level of explanation of reality,

---

[16] Munitz 186

LIMERICK COUNTY LIBRARY 0082037S

mechanism, is as described above. Meaning implies the purpose behind the mechanical motion and matter in the universe. So the explanatory power of mechanism and the explanatory power of meaning are at different levels of explanation.

Having now explored the two categories of the levels of explanation of reality, we can now employ the explanatory power of meaning as the tool for exploring the Agency level of reality.

The relationship between the two categories of the levels of explanation of reality is as follows:

1ST CATEGORY: MECHANISM / AGENCY LEVEL OF EXPLANATION

2ND CATEGORY: MECHANISM / MEANING LEVEL OF EXPLANATION

Let x represents mechanism, y represents agency and z represents meaning. Hence,

$$XY/XZ, \qquad \frac{XY}{XZ} = \frac{Y}{Z}$$

What the outcome of the above computational analysis represents is that why mechanism as an explanatory power is vital at some level of reality, that is, at the methodological reductionistic level, it takes the back seat at the ontological level, the agency level of explanation of reality, where the explanatory power of meaning as the tool for exploring the agency level of reality has a higher explanatory power.

As we've already established, the Agency level of reality is the deepest level of reality there is. To access reality at the deepest level, appeals to the supernatural agency are necessary. It is necessary to clarify that there are also categories at the agency level. There is the category of human agency as well as the category of supernatural agency.

First, we need to clarify what the category of human agency entails. The human agency is intricately linked to one's essence, one's essence being essentially what one is. It's important to understand one's sense of agency and how one exercises one's agency. One's sense of agency implies an exercise of it. Therefore one's sense of agency is being aware of how one's actions influence situations in one's circle of influence. This influence one exercises over situations in one's circle of influence has physiological and psychological ramifications.

Physiologically (with regards to the function of human body), the following analogy will suffice as an example of one's sense of agency or exercise of one's agency.

Suppose that a crowd of several thousand people gather in a football stadium to watch a football game, or in a theatre to watch a West End show or at a film premier to catch a glimpse of some film stars. Each of the spectators will be aware (sense of ownership) of which of the eyes or arms or legs in the room or at the arena are theirs. Likewise if any of the participants raises their arm to give another individual a hand shake, they will be aware (sense of agency) that it is their arm that performs the movement to reach out to another participant in the room or at the arena.

Psychologically, one's sense of agency can revolutionise one's thought life, to the end of being aware of how one's actions can positively influence whatever situations are within one's circle of influence. A human agent has an innate ability via her sense of agency to be proactive rather than being reactive to situations that occur within her circle of influence. Covey in The 7 Habits of Highly Effective People: Habit one, puts it thus:

"Proactive people focus their efforts on their Circle of Influence. They work on the things they can do something about: health, children, problems at work. Reactive people focus their efforts in the Circle of Concern--things over which they have little or no control: the national debt, terrorism, the weather. Gaining an awareness of the areas in which we expend our energies in is a giant step in becoming proactive." [17] Second, the category of supernatural

---

[17] Covey R Stephen, The 7 Habits of Highly Effective People, Simon & Schuster UK Ltd 1989, 2004 p.65

agency also requires some clarification. Hence, clarification of a few terms including spirituality, transcendence, immanence etc., is in order here.

What is spirituality to the spiritual conscious 21st Century

man? Spiritual belief or practice in the 21st century does not have the same meaning that it does for the traditional religious belief or practice. Amongst a significant population of Westerners who claim to be spiritual, spirituality will mean a range of things including transcendental meditation, the sense of the sublime - the inspiring, uplifting, moving experience they derive from their love of music or the aesthetic experience of being appreciative of great art or beauty and so on. Spirituality to me or to a theistic Christian is the spiritual connection with the supernatural Agent, in theological sense, God, the intelligence behind the universe.

In a Biblical context the words Spirit [18] and spirituality originated from Judeo-Christian tradition. The Apostle Paul as early as the first century, in the book of Romans (written between AD 56 and AD 58) expressly differentiated between being spiritual (that is, being

---

[18] In the Trinitarian conception of God, the Holy Spirit is the third personality of the Godhead. The Trinity (the three personalities of God - God the Father, God the Son and God the Holy Spirit are coequal and are one God. The Trinity equates, the one and only God. This is in line with the Belgic Confession thus: "Article 8: About the Holy Trinity of Persons in a Single Divine Essence Joined to this truth and the Word of God, we believe in one God alone (Who is one essence, with incommunicable properties in three persons, having had a real distinction of affairs from eternity), certainly in accordance with the Father, Son, and Holy Spirit. 1 John 2:10; Esa. 43:11; John 1:12, 1; 1 John 1:1; Apoc. 19:13; Prov. 8: 22; John 1:14. For the Father is the cause, origin, and beginning of all visible and invisible things. The Son is the Word, the Wisdom, and the Image of the Father. The Holy Spirit is the true power and strength that emanates from the Father and the Son. Nevertheless, this distinction does not make it that God is divided, as if into three parts, seeing that Scripture teaches us that the Father, the Son, and the Holy Spirit each has a hypostasis, or a subsistence, distinguished by their properties. Thus these three persons are nevertheless one God alone......."

influenced by the Spirit) and being sensual (corporeal or worldly) influenced by one's natural proclivity. The two terms, Spirit and spirituality conjure up a picture of God's essence. God is Spirit John 4:24. For our purposes here, being spiritual also has implications for being open to God the Holy Spirit, or appealing to the supernatural agent God in order to gain insight to the realm of the ultimate reality, as opposed to remaining sensual, that is, in the limited plane of partial natural reality that scientism engenders.

What is the transcendence / Immanence of the supernatural Agent, God? Cosmologically, the transcendence of God implies that the supernatural Agent, God exists outside of space and time and therefore as the First Cause brought the universe into existence. The immanence of God (which also has close correlation to God's omnipresence) implies that God exists within time and space. The sceptics (in the main, atheistic scientists and philosophers) generally argue against, the Christian theistic claim for the existence of the supernatural agent God, on the grounds of the confusion created by fragmented views held by Pantheists and deists.

THE DEFEAT OF THE SCEPTIC'S REBUTTAL AGAINST THE THEISTIC APPEAL TO THE SUPERNATURAL AGENCY

The sceptics argue to rebut the Christian theistic claim. The sceptics challenge Christian theists to show that they are not mistaken in their belief for the need to appeal to the supernatural Agent, God. This rebuttal will be responded to below.

The dual attribute of transcendence / immanence with regards to God's relation to His creation nailed the coffin of the bifurcation created by Pantheists on one hand, who believe, that everything is a part of God or everything is God which presupposes God's equality with His creation; and by deists on the other, who believe that God is separate from His creation but hold that God, though initiated creation has retired and is not now actively involved in it. Hence deistic and pantheistic positions on transcendence / immanence of the supernatural agent God suggest an 'Either / Or' proposition thus:

Deism: is asserting God's transcendence while rejecting His immanence.

Pantheism: is rejecting God's transcendence while asserting His immanence.

Pantheism and deism however, shoot themselves in the foot as the transcendence / immanence of the supernatural agent God is rather 'Both And' proposition.' This is so because the ultimate reality is that, God who is above His creation, is also actively involved in it.

The Christian theist is a step further here in justifying his appeal to the supernatural agent God. The Christian theist needs to respond to the sceptic on his rebuttal of the argument regarding an appeal to the supernatural agent God. The sceptic challenges the Christian theist to show that he is not mistaken in his belief for the need to appeal to the supernatural Agent, God. The first clarification here, is to establish that the sceptic has not refuted the Christian theists' argument for the existence of the supernatural agent God. That is, the sceptic has not shown or proved that the Christian theist's claim is false. The sceptic has only indicated the logical possibility that the Christian theist might be mistaken in his belief in the existence of the supernatural God as the theist has not proved his claim to be true. But neither could the sceptic prove that the Christian claim is false. So the Christian theist can respond that probabilistically speaking, he could be logically mistaken in his appeal to the supernatural agent God, but that the sceptic does not have an epistemic justification for his rebuttal of the Christian theist's claim, as the Christian theist has epistemic right to hold this belief. So the Christian theist can in turn rebut the sceptic's argument by asking him to show how that the Christian theist is wrong in his belief that the supernatural agent God exists. Since the sceptic is unsuccessful in either his rebuttal and or in refuting the Christian theist's argument for appealing to the supernatural agent God, we can resume our appeal to the supernatural agency in exploring meaning at the level of supernatural agency.

To summarise, so far we've established that explanation at the mechanistic level (methodological reductionism which is partial reality as explained by natural science) does not satisfy our curiosity about the ultimate reality.

We now make appeals to the supernatural agency level of the ultimate reality.

Here we seek to employ the explanatory power of meaning as the tool for exploring the supernatural agency level of reality that has a higher explanatory power.

Chapter 4

THE EXPLANATORY POWER OF MEANING AND APPEAL TO THE SUPERNATURAL AGENCY

The very reason why scientism, the notion that science is all knowledge there is, is false, is that it does not operate at the explanatory level of meaning, but merely a pragmatic, empirical phenomenon.

The explanatory power of meaning to my mind, is, key to understanding the realm of the ultimate reality. What is meaning? Meaning implies significance, worth or importance of something.

So in Christian theism, we speak of finding God as meaning, entering into a dynamic relationship with God, the source of life, life which finds expression in God's creative activities of the universe and of his eternal present and future kingdom.

In what sense does the natural science lack meaning? As aforementioned, the practice of our modern science is not a pursuit of truth but of a reliable knowledge. Empiricism which underpins the practice of modern science is the philosophical belief concerning sense derived knowledge. This is the philosophical belief that knowledge is all there is, (scientism) which is derived from the experience of the senses. If all knowledge is derived only from sensory experience, it follows by this logic that reality consists only of our sensory experience - our perceptual experience, the operation of our five senses, of hearing, touch, taste, smell and sight. But no one is in under any delusion, except of course, the scientismist, (someone who believes that science is all knowledge there is) that the senses are in any way, a commensurate test of reality.

Before further analysis of the exploratory power of meaning, here is a true story, the out of the box reflection of a scientific atheist, Chris Arnade [19] on what constitutes a meaningful outlook to

---

[19] Chris Arnade, The people who challenged my atheism most were drug addicts and prostitutes.   "Chris Arndade, theguardian.com".http://www.theguardian.com/commentisfree/2013/dec/24/atheism-richard-dawkins-challenge-beliefs-homeles(accessed 24/12/2013)

life beyond materialism. Chris' reflection was borne out of the personal encounter he had twice in his life with the genuine faith of destitute people, that we thoughtlessly, in my view, call the scum of the earth. The first time was in a workplace. He was a 16 year old student, doing a school holiday job to make ends meet. Other employees who though were addicted to drugs and poor had a noticeably genuine faith. These poor people would use every fifteen minutes break to read out of a torn bible and prayed. Chris described his proud attitude when one of these people called 'the preacher man' would challenge his atheism and invited him to believe in God thus:

"Preacher Man would question me, "What do you believe in?" I would decline to engage, out of politeness. He pressed me.

Finally I broke, I am an atheist. I don't believe in a God. I don't think the world is only 5,000 years old, I don't think Cain and Abel married their sisters!

Preacher Man's eyes narrowed. He pointed at me, "You are an APE-IEST. An APE-IEST. You going to lead a life of sin and end in hell."

"The second time that Chris met with people that the society commonly regarded as contemptible or worthless was when Chris had achieved a doctoral degree in physics and having pursued for over 20 years a successful career as a scientist on the Wall Street. Chris further described what happened during this time of his life thus:

"A life devoted to rational thought, a life devoted to numbers and clever arguments.

During that time I counted myself an atheist and nodded in agreement as a wave of atheistic fervor swept out of the scientific community and into the media, led by Richard Dawkins.

I saw some of myself in him: quick with arguments, uneasy with emotions, comfortable with logic, able to look at any ideology or any thought process and expose the inconsistencies. We all picked on the Bible, a tome cobbled together over hundreds of years that provides so many inconsistencies. It is the skinny 85lb (35.6kg) weakling for anyone looking to flex their scientific muscles."

Then came 'the eureka moment' for Chris, when he discovered the 'meaninglessness of atheism' but a 'meaningful contemplative Christian devotional life' led by his destitute colleagues with its associated confidence in God for facing cruel, cold devastating issues of life with a sense of triumph.

Chris had his second encounter with people who were destitute but exuded genuine strong faith in God, after he left his Wall Street job and started working with photographing homeless addicts in the South Bronx in the United States. Chris recorded his amazement thus:

"When I first walked into the Bronx I assumed I would find the same cynicism I had towards faith. If anyone seemed the perfect candidate for atheism it was the addicts who see daily how unfair, unjust, and evil the world can be. None of them are. Rather they are some of the strongest believers I have met, steeped in a combination of Bible, superstition, and folklore."

Chris' final analysis of 'presumption of atheism' and 'meaningfulness of theism' is instructive as to the highest capital that accrues to us via the explanatory power of meaning in exploring the ultimate reality by appealing to the supernatural agency. Chris being atheist himself honestly concluded his challenge to the flimsy reality that atheism holds compared to richness in supernatural agent God that Christian theism upholds thus:

"In these last three years, out from behind my computers, I have been reminded that life is not rational and that everyone makes mistakes. Or, in Biblical terms, we are all sinners.

We are all sinners. On the streets the addicts, with their daily battles and proximity to death, have come to understand this viscerally. Many successful people don't. Their sense of entitlement and emotional distance has numbed their understanding of our fallibility.

Soon I saw my atheism for what it is: an intellectual belief most accessible to those who have done well. I look back at my 16-year-old self and see Preacher Man and his listeners differently. I look at the fragile women praying and see a mother working a minimum wage custodial job, trying to raise three children alone. Her children's father off drunk somewhere. I look at the teenager fingering a small cross and see a young woman, abused by a father addicted to whatever, trying to find some moments of peace. I see Preacher Man himself, living in a beat up shack without electricity, desperate to stay clean, desperate to make sense of a world that has given him little.

They found hope where they could.

I want to go back to that 16-year-old self and tell him to shut up with the "see how clever I am attitude". I want to tell him to appreciate how easy he had it, with a path out. A path to riches.

I also see Richard Dawkins differently. I see him as a grown up version of that 16-year-old kid, proud of being smart, unable to understand why anyone would believe or think differently from himself. I see a person so removed from humanity and so removed from the ambiguity of life that he finds himself judging those who think differently. I see someone doing what he claims to hate in others. Preaching from selfish vantage point."

To further inform our understanding of where the issues lie with regards to how the exploratory power of meaning ties us to metaphysics or the ultimate nature of reality, we here examine the historical debate between the rationalists and the empiricists concerning reliability of our sense experience to gain knowledge of reality. Before Kant, in the 17th and 18th centuries this debate was amongst two set of philosophers - the continental rationalists, Descartes, Spinoza and Leibniz against the British Empiricists, Locke (though Locke was rationalistic in respect of our knowledge of God's existence), Berkeley and Hume. For our purposes here, the aspect of the debate we are concerned with is with regards to the opposing views held by rationalists and empiricists respectively on knowledge of truths about the ultimate reality (the external reality, the realm beyond our minds.) The claim made by empiricists about our knowledge of the external reality which consequently informs that of the present day empiricists (scientismists), is that, while reason may play a part in the process, experience ultimately is our sole information capital. The apparent implications are that the truths of the external reality can be known on the grounds of sense experience alone. The rationalists however claim that some truths of the external reality (external world) are known a priori and that this knowledge is of greater quality compared to any knowledge that mere experience can offer.

How has the exploratory power of meaning tied us to the external world or the external reality? Metaphysics as a philosophical discipline helps to answer this question, metaphysics being the branch of philosophy concerned with the fundamental nature of reality. Metaphysics originates from the work of Aristotle (384-322 B.C.) under the central themes of the 'study of being' and the 'study of first causes' which kick started the interest in the study of God as the first cause. The continental rationalists in the 17th and 18th centuries popularised the study of metaphysics which they categorised into general metaphysics - ontology and special metaphysics which covers cosmology, rational psychology and natural theology. We are most concerned here with issues of continued study in contemporary metaphysics, that is, ontology – the study of being or existence. In the academy today, issues in contemporary metaphysics that are addressed include mind-body problem, causality, nature of time and space, problem of free will and the meaning of a person. We are also interested in whether certain things exist, including properties, numbers, events, relations, souls, material objects and universals. And if they do, we ask, what are the characteristics of these things? For example, the question of whether the universals exist apart from their particulars that we observe in the physical world has been perennial since the time of the ancient Greeks.

The concept of universals originated from Plato's (428-348 B.C.) theory of Ideas or Forms. Plato asserted the existence of universals. That is, Plato's theory of Ideas functions as an explanatory theory of how the universal attributes of particular things are created by being modelled after their universal archetypes. To Plato the universals are transcendent (that is, universals are from above, and from the Christian theistic Christian worldview, from the supernatural realm.)

What are universals in relation to their particulars? Universals are things that can be instantiated or shared by different individual objects, for example Plato's 'Ideal man' in 'the transcendental world or realm' from whom different individual particulars we observe in the physical realm – John, Wane, Michael and so on, obtain their essence of humanness. Or Plato's ideal Chair in the transcendental world from which different individual particulars chairs – lecture room chairs, dining chairs, court room chairs and so on, obtain their identity of what it means to be a chair.

To appeal to the supernatural agency therefore, we need to assume a number of philosophical positions. We need to be realists, essentialists, dualists and transcendentalists.

Suppose we are realists about the existence of universals, then we assert that universals exist (in the external world or transcendental realm or realm of the Supernatural agency of spiritual entities) other than their particulars or particular things, the material things we observe in the physical world. So universals exist in the realm of the 'ultimate reality' from where they impact their particulars in the physical or material world. So I'm a realist about supernatural agents.

We are essentialists (we believe in the real existing essences) about the existence of universals, in the sense that we hold that universals are essences of individual particulars things, that is the archetypes or perfect models of those individual particular things. So the 'ideal man' or perfect model man is the essence of the individual particular man, for example, John, Wane, Michael and so on, that we observe in the physical material world. Also the 'Ideal chair' or perfect model chair as the universal gives meaning to the different individual particular chairs, for example, lecture room chairs, dining chairs, court room chairs etc., that we observe in the physical world.

This leads to our being dualists as we hold a position of there being dual worlds. That is, 'Ideal world' of the ultimate reality, the realm of the Supernatural agency and the 'material world' of mere physical reality.

Our being transcendentalist about universals presupposes that we hold that universals are supreme and belong to the highest realm that is above the physical world to which their particulars, for example a particular man or a particular chair or a particular table and so on, belong.

How do we ascend from our standpoint in the physical world

of materialism to the realm of ideas or transcendental realm? Or how do we gain knowledge of the realm of ideas from our standpoint in the realm of materialism? To Plato we assume a rationalistic outlook to knowledge (by reasoning our way from the physical realm to the realm of ideas) as opposed to empirical outlook via senses as discussed above.

Chapter 5

INTRODUCING TRANSCENDENTAL SEMIOTICS

I coin the term 'transcendental semiotics' to denote the study of semiotics in the transcendental realm – the 'spirit-sphere.' The cultural theorists make references to the public and private spheres. I here differentiate between the terrestrial sphere and the 'spirit-sphere.' The three phase development of the earth follows the order of the geosphere of the inanimate matter, the biosphere of the biological life and the notion of noosphere, the domain of the mind or the 'sphere of human cognition'. Here I make reference to the 'spirit-sphere' the domain of the supernatural agency. Being realist about supernatural entities – (God, angels even demons) connote that these entities really exist (in the external world or transcendental realm or realm of the Supernatural agency of spiritual entities) other than their particulars that we observe in the physical world

Semiotics is the study of signs. The concept of signs was proposed in the early 1900 by the Swiss Linguist Ferdinand de Saussure and the American Charles Pierce. Saussure defined a sign as composed of a two part model that he called the signifier and the signified. Pierce's model of sign consist of object (referent), representamen (which is equivalent in meaning to Saussure'signifier), and interptretant (equivalent in meaning to Saussure's signified).

The association of the signifier with the signified Saussure called signification. Pierce on the other hand developed three types of signs that he called icon, index and symbol. However, no sign has any meaning unless it is interpreted through the lens of its code in which the sign is engraved. That is, the meaning of a sign depends on the code in which it is located. Codes provide a vital framework within which signs have meaning or make sense. So it is the code engraved in the sign that gives the sign its meaning. In the 'spirit-sphere,' a sign is a spiritual entity, for example, God.

Within the transcendental semiotics, we have the signifiers-spiritual entities, and in the physical realm we have the signified – the physical objects. The idea here is that there is a connection between the signifier in the spirit-sphere and the objects that they signify in the physical realm.

Comparable to the Ideal world of Plato where universals (essences), for example 'Idea man' or Ideal Chairs or tables as essences really exist and instantiated as things in the material world as say particulars, for example, a particular man, a particular chair, a particular table.

So, there is a 'spirit-sphere' or spiritual realm where spiritual entities – signifiers - God, angels really exist and instantiated as the signified - Jesus - God incarnate, God-Man that dwelt with men on earth and a particular man created in God's image as the crown of God's creation.

TRANSCENDENTAL SEMIOTICS' SIGNIFERS AND SIGNIFIED

SIGNIFIERS	SIGNIFIED
God	Christ God-Incarnate,
	Particular man
Angel	Guardian Angel
Demons	Demonic influences

This process (semiosis according to Pierce) of interpreting a sign by referring to its object (referent) to produce meaning, is instructive for their being the ontological level (the place of God - sign), where the explanatory power of meaning as the tool for exploring the Supernatural agency level of reality has a higher explanatory power.

THE ONTOLOGICAL DIMENSION OF TRANSCENDENTAL SEMIOTICS

Ontologically, in the medieval metaphysics of an Aristotelian and Platonic conception of existence, the notion of being is mutually exclusive. A being is either necessary or contingent. In this sense and in line with the Christian theistic claim, God is a necessary Being. That is, God cannot but be, as God's non-being entails a contradiction in terms. By law of non contradiction it is impossible for A to be A and A to be non A at the same time. In Aristotle's words:

"one cannot say of something that it is and that it is not in the same respect and at the same time". [20]

So as Christian theists we have an ontological commitment that God exists, since our belief brings with it a rational commitment to the answer to the ontological question, does God exist? This we answer affirmatively. Our commitment here has historical root. In the 11th century, St. Anselm of Canterbury's ontological argument [21] for the existence of God is postulated on the proposition of 'a being for which no greater can be conceived.' The rationale is that non existence of such a being implies that 'a greater being' than 'a being for which no greater can be conceived' exists. The absurdity of this new conception is however obvious, as nothing can be greater than a being than which no greater can be conceived, hence, a being than which no greater can be conceived – God exists.

In my transcendental semiotics thesis therefore, the ontological status of the uncreated Personal God – 'the signifier' and the ontological status of the finite man - 'the signified' both imply that they are co-ontologically significant.[22]

To Baker (2002), Ontological significance is a feature of properties and a feature of things that have those properties thus: "(OS1) The property of being an F has ontological significance if and only if, necessarily, if x is an F (nonderivatively), then being an F determines x's persistence conditions.

(OS2) (Nonderivative) Fs have ontological significance in virtue of being Fs if and only if the property of being an F has ontological

---

[20] Aristotle, Metaphysics, the most quoted statement that represents the Aristotle's law of noncontradiction.

[21]Oppy, Graham, "Ontological Arguments", The Stanford Encyclopedia of Philosophy (Spring 2015 Edition) EdwardN.Zalta(ed.),URL= http://plato.stanford.edu/archives/spr2015/entries/ontological-arguments/> (Internet Accessed on 15 March 2014)

[22] In the transcendental semiotics sense and on the related theistic conception of meaning, man only finds meaning in being created in God's image.

significance." [23]

Their co-ontological significance derives from there being the universal – the uncreated Personal God, that is instantiated in the finite man created in God's image – the particular.

---

[23] Lynne Rudder Baker "The Ontological Status of Persons," Philosophy and Phenomenological Research 65 (2002): 370-388.

Chapter 6

MEANING, CONSCIOUNESS AND REALITY

So, meaning is vital to our exploration of the supernatural agency level of reality. We cannot but concede that reality is not only physical but immaterial as well. The philosophical argument for there being an agency level of reality is predicated on the raison d'être of there being a distinction between the physical reality and the non- physical (immaterial) reality. We all ought to hold the dichotomist worldview in relation to the physical reality and the non-physical (immaterial) reality. There is no neutral ground. On the physical realist's perspective, the physical reality is subject to physical laws, whilst on the immaterialist conception of reality, the immaterial reality is not subject to the constraints of the physical laws. Physical reality is evidentially clear to all as it can be empirically proven. What about immaterial reality? Immaterial reality is non-physical in terms of abstract phenomena such as consciousness, moral or ethical attributes such as goodness as opposed to evil proclivity and transcendental reality, the realm of the uncreated personal God and spirits as discussed above.

Exploring the transcendental level of reality here, presupposes appealing to the supernatural agency level of reality. This appeal requires the explanatory power of meaning as the tool for exploring the supernatural agency level of reality that has a higher explanatory power.

The explanatory power of meaning in turn, is, key, in understanding the realm of the ultimate reality.

To begin the daunting task of constructing the supernatural agency level of reality via the explanatory power of meaning, let's consider further attributes of the ultimate reality against the physical (material) reality. Plato's realm of the forms and Kant's Noumena (the thing-in-itself) are these philosophers' classical conceptions of the ultimate reality that corroborate the theistic conception of the transcendental realm of the ultimate reality. The realm of the forms or the nature of the theistic transcendental realm of the ultimate reality is eternal and unchanging in contradistinction with our sensory world of (material) reality which is subject to time and change.

These attributes, that is, the ultimate reality being 'eternal', and 'unchanging' are consequential for exploring the supernatural agency level of reality via the explanatory power of meaning, in contrast to the attributes of our sensory world of material reality being subject to time and change.

SENSORY WORLD	ETERNAL WORLD (ULTIMATE REALITY)
Subject to Time & Change	Eternal & Unchanging

WHAT'S THE NATURE OF CONSCIOUSNESS?

To my mind the reason that man can't fully explain 'consciousness,' why the phenomenon is elusive to the human mind is parallel to the reason why the 'higher consciousness' – God the source of human consciousness, is indefinable to man -the reason why man can't fully explain the supernatural agent God.

Plato gave us an insight into what the ultimate reality of consciousness looks like with his theory of forms, the realm of 'ideal' as aforementioned. In this vein, the immaterial reality can be said to be clothed by the physical reality. So for an observable object say a sentient human creature - man, from naturalistic evolutionary perspective, may simply be defined by his bio-chemical, anatomic composition or properties - body mass, human molecular formula etc. This naturalistic assumption implies that human beings are just a bunch of chemicals working about in bags. In Kant's Noumena / Phenomena divide however, the physical reality is definitely an artificial 'cover' of the 'thing-in- itself' rather than what the thing actually is. The thing-in -itself represents the ultimate reality. The word cover here is instructive, being the act of masking, the concealing of the existence of the 'thing-in-itself' by obstructing the view of it. To understand what consciousness is, our task becomes that of uncovering of the 'thing-in-itself' in order to reveal the ultimate reality.'

On definitional note, consciousness is on two levels:

Scientifically and subjectively personal defined consciousness.

There is the scientifically defined consciousness which posits consciousness as an epiphenomenon of brain activities. This empiricist's conception of reality entails materialism and the two combined presupposes an eliminativist conception of spiritual reality, that there is no spiritual reality but only material reality in which all that exists is in space and time. The proponents of the eliminativist conception of spiritual reality will have us believe that as we live in a universe of mass, energy, space and time, consciousness is nothing more than what originates from the complex systems of our brain. In summation, the eliminativist view completely rules out the existence of the mind in favour of an absolutivist view of matter – matter is all there is. With regards to the brain, the scientific stand point is that consciousness is nothing more than the firing of the 10billions of neurons that the brain of an individual person mainly consists of. This however, is only a scratching of the surface of the problem of consciousness, a tip of the ice berg, which in the academy is known as the easy problem of consciousness.

The easy problem of consciousness aligns squarely with the concept of emergence (the scientific claim that consciousness is an emergent property of the brain) or the notion of correlation (the scientific / philosophical view with regards to an association of consciousness with the brain.) For example, consciousness is explained scientifically in terms of its correlation to brain function – how the brain affects consciousness, an attempt to find out what goes on in the brain when we solve a complex mathematical problem, have a thought, or have an experience.

Each of the ten billions of neurons of the human brain is a mechanism for transporting information from one part of the brain to another. It's therefore arguable that experiments in neuroscience via fMRI (functional magnetic resonance imaging) do no more than mapping images of changing blood flow in the brain associated with neural activity. In this regard fMRI is functional only in detecting brain structures and processes which may be associated with perception, thought and action. There is a consensus in the academy that we will probably in the future understand these phenomena.

Attempts have been made in scientific experiments to force

the issue that some perceptual consciousness related Christian spiritual experiences such as a belief in a supernatural God emerges only from the brain activities. Such experiments examine the brain electrical / chemical activities in the brain of individuals involved via brain scanning to determine how the brain is functionally responsible for people's act of 'believing' or when they pray to the conclusion that neuroscience has disproved God. It's however inconceivable that such experiences are resolvable scientifically.

This leads us to the hard problem of consciousness that presupposes that the gap that the perennial mind / body problem created, is yet to be bridged. So, if we take two features of consciousness, thought and memory, we find for example, that we are yet to discover what thought is. Thought can't be put down to a molecular or chemical formula. Neuroscience also admits that the state of the earth research on memory suggests that why neuroscience claims to have an inkling of the molecules, chemicals and neurons that may be involved in the composition of this enigma, neuroscience has no clue what memory actually is. [24]

One wonders then that despite most scientists' above admission of cluelessness with regard to the hard problem of consciousness that the new atheists including Sam Harris, Daniel Dennett, Richard Dawkins and so on, are bent on their physicalist view of reality by being eliminative about consciousness. Also one cannot but ask with regard to the hard problem of consciousness as David Chalmers put it:

"How does something as immaterial as consciousness arise from something as unconscious as matter?"

This thought provoking question and its implications for the long standing mind / body problem which in the academy is believed to remain unresolved, logically leads one to view the new atheists' physicalist stance as untenable. On my 'levels of explanation' thesis, the physicalists are confusing levels of explanation of reality in their assertion that consciousness is nothing but only activities in the brain.

Given the intractable nature of consciousness, it's hard to see how

---

[24] The God Question DVD series www.thegodquestion.tv

scientific explanation can ever lead us to the truth of the immaterial fundamental nature of reality that human consciousness is. Our scientific tools –fMRI cannot detect immaterial features of human consciousness – that is, awareness in form of our experience of perception, feeling, thought, memory, imagination etc.

Free Will.

A contentious and closely related issue to scientifically defined consciousness is free will which in turn is linked to a hotly philosophical debated issue of morality which has implications for our view of responsibility and guilt.

We may ask, are we 'in control' or 'not in control?

On one hand, the traditional kind of freewill is the libertarian view of freewill, the kind that is rife amongst the general populace. The libertarian view of freewill is the view that as conscious beings we are in control of our will and responsible for our actions. This is mainly the general Judeo - Christian theistic position.

On the other hand, determinism is a view that our conscious self is not in control of our decisions. This view in the main is the atheistic position which could be compatibilist or incompatibilist. Compatibilism implies that we can still have free will despite our decisions being determined. The determinist and incompatibilist position is the deterministic view that is incompatible with the traditional view of freewill of the libertarian persuasion. This is the position of Sam Harris as expressed in his 2012 book "Freewill". The determinist and compatibilist position however alludes to the compatibility of determinism with freewill. Our freewill under the determinist and compatibilist position is causally determined. This is the notion that we can be free and causally determined. In this sense, determinism is compatible with freewill. This is the position of Michael Ruse who is a causal determinist and Daniel Dennett who has condemned Harris' determinist and incompatibilist position, in his review of Harris' 2012 book "Free Will". The determinist and compatibilist position begs the question as to whether, if we subscribe to the libertarian position, we are suffering from what is called in the academy an illusion of Free Will.

So we ask, what's responsible for decisions that we make, is it the conscious us (via our freewill, implying we are in control) or the unconscious transactional activities taking place in our brain, over which we can exercise no control? Benjamin Libet was the pioneering scientist to conduct experiments resulting in how researchers now attempt to detect and predict (via functional magnetic resonance imaging (fMRI) that the unconscious electrical processes in the human brain are responsible for making decisions before the subjects of such experiments are conscious of having made those decisions. Sam Harris relying on the so called evidence from experiments in neuroscience holds hard determinism and would want us believe that physical determinism is true and so render free will impossible. But how conclusive is the evidence from such neuro-scientific experiments? To date, the evidence should be taken with the pinch of salt, as it cannot be said to be conclusive.

The researchers of the experiments like Harris believe the outcome of the experiments reveal equivocally, that the thought of the subjects of the experiment equates their brain activity, meaning, the consciousness of the subject of these experiments is encoded in their brain activity, leading only to one conclusion that is mechanistically determined, hence we have no control over our decisions, we have no free will. This deterministic view supposedly implies that dualism between the conscious mind and the brain activity is non-existent, a kind of a bridge for the known dualistic nature of the mind / matter divide. The assertion of this view by Professor John-Dylan Haynes, [25] amongst others of the same persuasion including Jerry Coyne for instance, raises more questions than it answers. So we may further ask, Is, our sense of free will illusory? Are we agents of action or products of causes in the brain? Are our decisions predicated on some model of the mind or the model of human nature? Do our decisions emanate from our consciousness (i.e. our agency is responsible for our actions) or are our decisions predetermined that is, a product of physical processes in the brain (i.e. we do not have

---

[25] John-Dylan Haynes of the Bernstein centre for computational neuroscience Berlin. Neuroscience & Freewill THE \Y\OUTUE VIDEO of the experiment – on neuroscience and free will – stated that the subject of the experiment's brain predicted 7 seconds before he consciously made his decision of choosing left or right. https://www.youtube.com/watch?v=N6S9OidmNZM

control over our actions)?

The above questions that represent an indiscriminate notion that humans as well as all other objects in the material world are all essentially machines and predetermined and so are predicated on the causal determination of the universe, is a grossly inadequate one

In contradistinction to the thesis of one system of knowledge / truth that is postulated in this work, the 'determined will' notion presumes a fragmented system of knowledge / truth, in which every action can only be explained by every causal action that precedes it. This narrow minded perspective to the nature of reality posits 'my way or the high way' approach to understanding everything in terms of causal determinism without exception. It is a strawman argument that commits a fallacy of fragmentation of knowledge / truth, thus:

1. We live in a physical / material universe where every phenomenon is causally determined.

2. Our decisions are brought about by the brain state.

3. Therefore our sense of free will is an illusion.

My critique of the foregoing is the following. The above fallacious argument in its attempt to validate the fragmentation of our knowledge / truth of causality or causation couldn't be more wrong. The linearity or one dimensional conception of causality, that, the deterministic worldview posits, in which the universe is nothing more than a chain of events that follow one after the other in line with the law of cause and effect, is a misguided view of reality of causality.

Causal determinism leads to an infinite regress of causes. So to determine the truth of proposition P1 that our consciousness is caused by neural activities in the brain, we must ask, what is the justification for these deterministic views or reasons? For the reasons (the inconclusive evidence) that material eliminativists have so far produced to count as knowledge, the evidence (that is, P1) must be justified with reasons P2, and the reasons P2 must be justified with the reasons P3, and so on, ad infinitum, why a physical causal deterministic reasons (that is, neurons in the brain) are the only and valid reasons responsible for our decision making capability.

Apparently, causal determinism in this regard stifles innovative means of investigating the nature of reality of consciousness. The determinstic approach can only lead us nowhere fast.

The above argument also over assumes that causality / causation is only physical. This reasoning arises from the conventional perception of causality / causation as the relation between an event (the cause) and a phenomenon (the effect), in which the phenomenon is conceived as the physical consequence of the event. A close study of the nature of causality however, leads to our understanding of causality / causation being not only physical but equally immaterial.

So what is the immaterial nature of causality? The Aristotelian philosophy posits the nature of causality as immaterial by inferring a first mover. The hard determinist however argues by asking, what caused the first mover? To this question the Aristotelian philosopher responds with Aristotle's original conception of the first mover, that the first mover is an unmoved mover. It is at least a logical possibility that the unmoved mover has thus broken the causal chain in a series of causes and effects (the infinite regress posited by causal determinism as depicted above). The influence of the Aristotelian philosophy has a far reaching impact on the eminent early empiricist Bacon Francis who is known as the father of scientific method or experimental science. Rather than causal influence being only physical the Aristotelian philosophy conceives the word 'cause' in terms of an explanatory answer to a 'why' (or metaphysical) question.

The existence of immaterial reality therefore presupposes a level of explanation that entails, in my view, metaphysical thinking. In this regard, 'why is there something rather than nothing' one famous and contestable question that scientists, theologians and philosophers have wrestled with since Leibniz posed it in the 17th century, speaks at least to immaterial reality of causality / causation. The question cries out for an answer that undoubtedly entails metaphysical reasoning. As Jim Holt [26] perceptibly conceived it,

---

[26] Jim Holt: Why does the universe exist? https://www.ted.com/talks/jim_holt_why_does_the_universe_exi st? language=en (accessed on 14 Jan 2015).

that whether reality is nothing or everything, it nevertheless demands an explanation. Lawrence Krauss's claim in his 2012 book, 'A Universe from Nothing' that preposterously suggests that the answer to this question, finds explanation in the scientific laws of quantum mechanics, period, case closed, end of story, is arrogant and laughable. Krauss actually believes that the question 'why?' is stupid, that it should rather be rendered 'How? But how wise is this remark about Leibniz the philosopher and mathematician to whom we are indebted, for being genius enough to invent the system of calculus? Not wise at all. David Albert, [27] a quantum theory expert in his critic of Krauss's book has asked wisely thus:

'Where, for starters, are the laws of quantum mechanics themselves supposed to have come from? Krauss is more or less upfront, as it turns out, about not having a clue about that. '

Perception of Jim Holt plus David Albert on being cautious and so not rush to a closed scientific inference to a more profound question such as 'why is there something rather than nothing' is wise without question. It is wise because this "why" question arguably has a scope for metaphysical reasoning. So we can conclude that causality / causation is not only physical but equally immaterial.

If causality / causation is immaterial, we have grounds for rebutting the hard determinist's claim that our decisions are predetermined as a product of physical processes in the brain. This is the claim that we do not have control over our actions and that our sense of free will is illusory. Having rebutted the hard determinist claim, on immateralist conception of causality / causation, we are justified in claiming that we are agents of our actions.

That is, our agency is responsible for our actions. We have free will and our decision emanate from our consciousness. Hence:

Philosophically, we argue for free will thus:

1. On the immaterialist conception of causality /

[27] Philosopher David Albert's critique of Krauss's book in The New York Times Book Review. Publish: March 23, 2012. (accessed on 22 Feb 2015).

causal influence is immaterial.

2. As we are agents of our actions, our agency is responsible for our actions.

3. Therefore, we have free will.

Philosophically, we also argue for consciousness thus:

1. Our decisions are predicated on the model of the mind.

2. We have control over our actions.

3. Therefore, our decisions emanate from our consciousness.

So, in line with my thesis of one system of knowledge based on a coherence system of truth, the hard determinists need to move away from the mindset, the default position that consciousness is solely an epiphenomenon of brain activities. The conception of consciousness as an incidental by product of the psychological events in the brain. The apparent incoherent view of consciousness that hard determinism entails, is an inkling to its rejection by compatibilism and indeed libertarianism which warmly embraces agent causation. The incoherence of hard determinism as an argument for sole account for our consciousness, is, where the problem lies, as far as my thesis of one system of knowledge is concerned.

Hard determinism paints this picture of consciousness, solely, from the scientific point of view. Of course I'm pro science and I welcome scientific contributions to finding answers to questions relating to reality of deeply mysterious phenomenon we call consciousness. The assumption of cognitive science (science of the mind), is that we can now get inside the human mind to undertake science of information processing in the brain. The snag is, that, some cognitive scientists also now called cognitive neuroscientists, conceive consciousness as mere neural correlates of the brain state. Our attempts involving scientific description of consciousness however should not be mistaken for an explanation of consciousness.

Currently, the scientific attempts to discover consciousness include scholarly proposals involving quantum theories of consciousness based on quantum mechanics. Jeffery M. Schwartz et al., in their article provide justification for the quantum theory of consciousness thus:

" Quantum theory must be used in principle because the behavior of the brain depends sensitively upon atomic, molecular and ionic processes, and these processes in the brain often involve large quantum effects". [28]

The concept of quantum theory of consciousness generally posits consciousness as arising from the fundamental level of the natural order, the unified field. So there are layers of nature that consist in the basic level, the molecular level, the atomic level, sub atomic level all arising from the unified field which contains codes that structure the other layers of nature. This is of course debatable. Is consciousness just the so called unified field hypothesis?

On the cognitive neuroscience front, attempts to discover consciousness involve the current extensive use of functional brain imaging technology such as EEG and especially fMRI, to measure neural correlates of consciousness (NCC). FMRI is expected to measure the neural correlates of the mental events in the brain. With regards to consciousness, the empirical approach is used to find out how the brain is able to produce a conscious experience. This is the sense in which the science of consciousness is expected to empirically depict the nature and relationship between the brain states and our subjective mental states.

Compared to the convention, whereby psychologists have relied on behavioural correlates, FMRI has proved to be a more objective attempt to measure our mental states. The critique of FMRI is with regard to being more a measure of secondary physiology rather than a direct qualitative measure of correlates of neural activities in the

_____._____

[28] Jeffrey M. Schwartz, Henry P. Stapp, Mario Beauregard. QUANTUM PHYSICS IN NEUROSCIENCE AND PSYCHOLOGY A NEUROPHYSICAL MODEL OF MIND/BRAIN INTERACTION. Section 5.2. p. 31 http://www.newdualism.org/papers/H.Stapp/Stapp-PTB6.htm (accessed on 4 March 2015).

brain.

In cognitive neuroscience, the amount of consciousness or level of awareness we can generate, corresponds to our level or state of consciousness. Our level of awareness / non awareness ranges from being at a vigilant state of consciousness when we are fully awake and are self-aware (when we are aware that we are aware), to being in Rapid Eye Movement (REM) sleep (dreaming state with little or no self-awareness) or deep sleep when we are fully asleep with no consciousness.

Clinically in the traditional fashion, patients are said to be in an impaired state of consciousness, for example, when they may have suffered brain damage and are in a locked in state, coma state, the Persistent (Continuing) Vegetative State or Minimally Conscious State (MCS). The state here denotes the degree of external or physical consciousness ranging from seemingly total absence of consciousness in a coma state, the Persistent (Continuing) Vegetative State and general anaesthesia to a Minimally Conscious State (MCS), the unsteady, somewhat limited consciousness being experienced by a sleep walker or someone in an epileptic seizure.

The new ground breaking research in neuroscience is however, redefining the aforementioned 'disorders of consciousness' into a new category of consciousness for people in a coma state or a persistent vegetative state. In the past, coma and persistent vegetative states were seen as indefinite states of unconsciousness, where a person is perceived to be unresponsive not only to his environment but also unresponsive cognitively to any stimulation including pain. The increasing use of techniques such as Positron Emission Tomography (PET) and functional magnetic resonance imaging (fMRI) has led to detecting how electrical activities in the brains of coma and persistent vegetative state patients are responding to instructions given by researchers, as demonstrated in the work of neuroscientist Adrian Owen. About 20 percent of the persistent vegetative state patients involved in the experiments seem to be responding via their brainwaves to instructions that ask them to imagine playing tennis or navigating rooms in their house. The new research has led to definition of a new category of consciousness. The new category of consciousness is useful in determining coma and persistent vegetative patients that are unconscious, those that present the usual coma / persistent vegetative state characteristics but are conscious and those that are in between.

The new research does have both diagnostic and ethical implications. So, when people are in coma or persistent vegetative state, it becomes unethical for clinicians to simply assume they are unconscious. To carry out an effective and meaningful diagnosis of coma and persistent vegetative states, clinicians will have to inquire into whether these patients fall into the following categories: Are they unable to communicate at all? Are they actually conscious but unable to communicate verbally? Or are they capable of responding only via their brainwaves? In the last category, our fMRI techniques may be able to address their communication issues. FMRI may be used (not mainly as a measure of a level of consciousness) as a means of communicating with people in a persistent vegetative state. Adrian Owen, a neuroscientist at The Brain and Mind Institute, Canada, claims that these experiments are useful and are producing a positive response.

On ethical grounds, the new research is making medical professionals to have a rethink on what constitutes life or death. In light of the new category of consciousness, many of them are cautious not to rush into conclusion that being on a life support machine, means being dead predictably. Possibility of patients gradually recovering from a persistent vegetable state to at least a minimally conscious state is increasingly being given a much needed moral consideration in the care of these patients. There is now an awareness of a two dimensional recovery model from a persistent vegetative state. One dimension of the model covers a possible recovery of consciousness with anecdotal evidence (people recovering after up to a decade in a persistent vegetative state) of awareness of one self and one's environment including interacting with other people and becoming responsive to both visual and auditory stimuli. The other dimension of the model covers a possible recovery of function resulting in being mobile (restoration of motor skills), being able to communicate verbally and in some cases, patients returning to paid employment. This is a testimonial to the resilient nature of the human being.

The most mysterious state of consciousness, to my mind, is

regarding the where about of a person's consciousness when they are under general anaesthesia that I call anaesthetics wonder. Even the medical profession doesn't understand how anaesthetics works, on top of our not understanding exactly what consciousness is. To provide some kind of description of what is going on, in a person's transition from a state of consciousness before anaesthetics is administered and a state of total unconsciousness after anaesthetics is administered, the neuroscientists are now able to capture the neural correlates of consciousness, in terms of observing changes in the patient's brain function. But that is as far as it goes.

So what's the link between Anaesthesia and consciousness? Has fMRI helped to establish a link between the state of anaesthesia and consciousness, by imaging the brain or put it another way, by recording the brain's electrical activity during anaesthesia? So far our clever brain imaging techniques have failed to unlock the deeply mysterious realm of our consciousness. The nearest to detecting which parts of the brain are influenced by anaesthetics to produce a state of unconsciousness in us when we are under, is the mapping of the changes in blood flow to different parts of the brain, resulting in a picture of so many parts that are deactivated by anaesthetics. This renders the results unpredictable as a pointer to the main cause of unconsciousness when we are under the influence of anaesthetics. The outcome of this technological inquiry, is, of course, the same for patients in a coma and persistent (continuing) vegetative state as for patients under anaesthetics. There is however a difference from a state of unconsciousness that results in being in a coma or in a persistent vegetative state and the anaesthetic (or drugs) induced unconsciousness. The former is involuntarily brought about by circumstances beyond the patient's control (a medical condition, accident resulting in brain damage etc.), the latter however, is, in a class of its own. In this case, by administering drugs to the patient, anaesthetists are able to lead the patient into a limbo, out of consciousness, in order to perform an operation, working internally with a scalpel within the patient body, and the patient experiencing no sense of pain at all, and when the operation is done bring the patient back to consciousness. Amazing.

What is the state of limbo that the patient under anaesthetics is in? The word limbo here, is not used in terms of conception of a place between heaven and hell. The state of limbo here, is the zone between 'aware' existence, before anaesthetics is administered and 'unaware' existence, when one is under the influence of anaesthetics. 'Aware' is a reference to being aware of one self and one's environment.

Research in neuroscience on consciousness and drug induced unconsciousness dwells on the information processing function of our brain. When we are conscious, the communication network in our brain ensures the synthesis and integration of information within different parts of the brain. This is more akin to the so called Global Workspace theory of consciousness. Thinking about sensory perception subjectively, seems simplistic, as it happens outside of our conscious awareness. For example, if I receive a sensory information of seeing a red apple, according to the global workspace theory, this sensory input is first processed within local regions of my brain without my awareness of it. I only become conscious of experiencing red apple if the sensory signals are broadcast via a network of neurons that fire, in synchrony all over my brain. It is this firing of the neurons in synchronising fashion that the global workspace theory regards as consciousness. When we are under anaesthesis (unconscious) however, a communication breakdown occurs in the neural network that signals the cessation of synthesis of information between different parts of the brain. As George Mashour [29] confirmed, some scientists have therefore postulated that the information processing in terms of the synthesis of the sensory inputs amongst different regions of the brain, is, what consciousness is! That is a very bold claim.

It's an understatement, to say that this assertion doesn't seem to have addressed the hard problem of consciousness. It's inconceivable that the assertion has even begun to scratch the surface of the hard problem of consciousness. The hard problem of consciousness relates to finding solution to what constitutes our conscious subjective experiences. By the way, our conscious subjective experiences are not just only sensory experiences, but

---

[29] George Mashour, anaesthetist at the University of Michigan in Ann Arbor   www.nytimes.com/.../what-**anesthesia**-can-teach-us-about-**consciousness**....10 Dec 2013 New York Times 10 December 2013.

include at deeper levels, perceptions, qualia (feelings, of subjective, personal and intimate experience,) imaginations, memory, intuition, cognitive (intelligent experiences) and higher order consciousness entailing spiritual experiences.

So in our search for what consciousness really is, one may ask, is research such as the Human Brain Project (HBP) that is geared towards the computational model, the simulation of the human brain, in terms of its computational functions, the way forward to uncovering the deeply mysterious human consciousness? It's unlikely that our quest for knowledge of what consciousness is will lead to any concrete discovery with the Human Brain Project (HBP). I'm not the only sceptic here. Many in the neuroscience community who initially were enthusiastic about the project were at a point quite concerned that the project 'is doomed to failure'. [30]

These critics threatened to boycott it in their complaint to the European Commission, the sponsor of the project. There are two interesting points made in the Guardian article by the project's leading supporters. Richard Frackowiak posits the simulation of the brain that the project aims to achieve as an inevitable "paradigm shift" in neuroscience and Henry Markram, the former head of the Human Brain Project affirmed the project's goal as an ICT project rather than a neuroscientific endeavour. [31] So the two current state of the art research approaches on the activities of the human brain, though, regard the brain as mainly an information processing organ, both nevertheless, are diametrically opposed in their aspirational goals. One – neuroscience, is still enthusiastically engaged in an ongoing scientific research that is orientated towards hard determinism, a rigid assertion, for example, that consciousness is the neural correlates of the brain state. The thesis of the human Brain Project, however, is geared towards moving the frontier of the brain sciences beyond just the brain's information processing function to utilisation of the massive data already generated by neuroscience to undertake super computer simulations of the human

_____

[30] Ian Sample, Scientists threaten to boycott € 1.2bn Human Brain Project. The Guardian, Monday 7 July 2014. www.theguardian.com › Science › Neuroscience, (accessed on 10 Dec 2014)
[31] Ian Sample, Scientists threaten to boycott € 1.2bn Human Brain Project.

brain. This attempt represents as asserted above by Richard Frackowiak, a radical paradigm shift in neuroscience. I believe this is a salient point that the scientific community, is yet to pay a due attention to. Further analysis shall be carried out of the paradigm shift that Frackowiak alluded to, and the implications of Markram's stated sole purpose for the HBP, as mainly computational, a super scale simulation of the entire human brain. Could this possibly lead to an explanatory project in academia of what consciousness is?

Before this analysis, as my thesis implies 'the unity of knowledge', it is in order, to introduce an insight from the social sciences, of what makes the human species who we are.

The general assumption, in the scientific community, is that evolution alone shapes the human behavioural disposition. There is evidence however, from anthropological studies to suggest that there is another offer as to what structures our behaviour. The rigid assertions made in the field of evolutionary psychology, sociobiology, etc., with regards to the evolutionary outlook to the nature of our behaviour, is now being challenged by alternative, flexible explanation for the structure of behaviour of the human species in relation to its environment. Everett (2015) an anthropologist developed two models regarding the human condition in order to differentiate the 'rigidity hypothesis 'from 'flexibility cognition'. Rigidity hypothesis [32] characterises the hard deterministic view that is rooted in solely evolutionary perspective to human behaviour, whereas, the human experience depicts that we develop, more flexibly as we are shaped by our cultural environment behaviourally. Everett put it aptly thus:

'In a species like Homo sapiens, with fewer genes than corn, the evidence supports the thesis that culture exerts a much stronger influence on human thought and behaviour than biology.'

---

[32] Daniel Everett, **Dark Matter of the Mind.** Daniel Everett. Dean of Arts and Sciences at Bentley University, anthropologist best-known for multiple decades spent with the Piraha people in the Amazon. iai The Institute of Art and ideas. Accessed on 25th March 2015.

In the controversy over the HBP's viability before the reorganisation was achieved through mediation to get the project back on track with the appointment of board of directors, what divides the cognitive scientists and the project leadership then goes beyond what meets the eye. At the fundamental level, the difference is conceptual. The project leadership seemed to see the neuroscientists as 'rigid cognizers' whereas, the project leaders saw themselves as 'flexible cognizers' who wish to see the implementation of the much needed paradigm shift in neuroscience.

PROPOSAL FOR IMPLEMENTATION OF THE THESIS

As a proposal of how my thesis of 'One system of knowledge' within a coherent system of truth, might be implemented in the academy, I'm introducing the concept of epistemic communities. This concept of epistemic communities is derived from the concept of scientific communities.

Thomas Kuhn (1962) in The Structure of Scientific Revolutions introduced the concept of "scientific communities" and how scientists go about practice of science within their individual communities. My construct of "epistemic communities", that might be developed, therefore covers wider "intellectual community" of disciplines other than, but include "scientific communities." The wider intellectual community, includes for example, theological, philosophical as well as scientific communities and so on.

The proposal here, entails a multidisciplinary practice towards an epistemic maximisation of truth', For example, in our search to find out what the deeply mysterious phenomenon called consciousness is, we can suppose that consciousness is two things propositionally thus:

1. Consciousness is the brain state.

2. Consciousness is, more subjectively, a phenomenon to be the brain state.

These two propositions represent two worldviews namely: the empirical, scientific view and the more subjective, holistic view respectively.

The intellectual community comprising of multidisciplinary bodies can then begin to collaboratively tackle the hard problem that is posed by the question of what consciousness really is, rather than just the hard deterministic naturalists belligerently imposing their views on the rest of the intellectual community, as often is currently the case.

For this collaboration to yield fruitful outcomes, members of the intellectual communities will have to abide by a set of 'multidisciplinary practice' ground rules including empathetic understanding, mutual respect, active listening and so on.

Borrowing a leave from Kuhn who made a landmark contribution to what we know scientifically in his book 'The Structure of Scientific Revolutions', I'm proposing here, a development of a 'Manual For Practice Of Epistemic Maximization Of Truth' within such epistemic communities; from ground breaking, developmental, multidisciplinary work by diverse scientific, theological, philosophical, psychological endeavors, toward maximization of truth.

Kuhn's book [33] depicts how new ideas in science are generated and gradually win acceptance amongst scientists. To Kuhn, there are three different periods of scientific activities that we can observe within the scientific communities thus:

Preparadigmatic stage: The stage when the scientific community is involved in discussion about the likelihood of a new paradigm emerging - the embryonic stage for an evolving paradigm. The early stages of the development of the ideas of the DNA project, the Human Genome project or the current project, the Human Brain (HBP) project as initiated by Henry Markram are good examples of prepardigmatic stage.

Normal science: is when a paradigm dominates science conducted within a given period which involves problem solving. This is the current stage of the European Human Brain Project. Revolutionary science is when the old paradigm is replaced by a new "paradigm." The old paradigm is challenged when someone in a scientific community is engaged in a new thinking about how things could be done differently. That is, there is a need for the paradigm to shift as it becomes certain that the current scientific information has become obsolete and needs to change. For example, the "Copernican revolution" [34] regarding planetary systems. To Kuhn, old tricks die

---

[33] Thomas S, Kuhn, The Structure of Scientific Revolutions. 2d ed. Chicago: University of Chicago Press, 1970

[34] To Thomas Kuhn, the Sun-centred or heliocentric model of our solar system, accepted within the scientific communities as "the Copernican Revolution," a paradigm shift from the Earth-centred Ptolemaic model of the planetary system, is a scientific revolution.

hard, and it is often the new generation of scientists that take the initiative to challenge the status quo. That is, normal science, the old paradigm that the old generation of scientists, fight tooth and nail to defend. This explains the controversy that ensued between the neuroscientists and the insistence by the initial HBP leaders, that the project is mainly an ICT project and that the project requires a much needed paradigm shift in neuroscience. [35]

KUHN'S PARADIGM SHIFT AND IMRE LAKATOS' METHODOLOGY OF SCIENTIFIC RESEARCH PROGRAMMES

The central theme of Kuhn's thesis in the structure of scientific revolutions, is, the concept of a paradigm shift. A paradigm, in this context, is a collection of beliefs and techniques that are shared by every member of a scientific community. That is, a scientific standard practice that every member of a scientific community can appeal to. Examples include Newton's universal law of gravitation, Darwin's origin of the species and so on.

Kuhn refuted the status quo and argued that there is no absolute scientific truth, rather scientific truths are relative. In other words they are subject to change as new paradigms replace the old ones to revolution science.

Kuhn, in the structure of scientific revolutions discussed the practice of normal science with subsequent paradigm shifts through scientific revolutions within various scientific communities, leading to a maximisation of our knowledge of various scientific fields. I am here advocating for a construct of epistemic communities (scientific, philosophical, theological and so on, for an epistemic maximization of truth, leading to unity of knowledge.

We owe the concept of paradigm shift to Kuhn. He asserted that scientific progress is often impeded by dogmatic stance of older generation of scientists who are often stuck in doing normal science as an objective way of going about things. They adamantly oppose

---

[35] Ian Sample, Scientists threaten to boycott € 1.2bn Human Brain Project.

change as they believe that the truth of science is objective. Karl Popper of the old paradigm school of mature or normal science believed that scientific knowledge is cumulative. Hence, there is a need for dogmatic adherence to scientific method. Kuhn however proposed a different form of dogma in normal science – a dogma in scientific paradigm.

Imre Lakatos refuted Kuhn's concept of scientific revolution and argued that scientific revolution occurs when scientists opt for a progressive research programme over a degenerating research programme:

"Now, Newton's theory of gravitation, Einstein's relativity theory, quantum mechanics, Marxism, Freudianism, are all research programmes, each with a characteristic hard core stubbornly defended, each with its more flexible protective belt and each with its elaborate problem-solving machinery." [36]

For the purposes of the work undertaken here however, I shall stick to Kuhn's concept of paradigm shifts as indicators of the structure of scientific revolutions. In my view this concept is closer to reality depicted in history and philosophy of science. The concept of paradigm shift is also, applicable to transformations that are observable in the history and philosophy of other disciplines as well.

IS SCIENTIFIC TRUTH ABSOLUTELY OBJECTIVE?

It is easier for generation of new scientists to be flexible and easily go along -with a new paradigm. In the words of Anthony Flew (2007), 'where the evidence leads'.

Scientists with an 'older generation perception' that operates within 'rigidity hypothesis' [37] who have always interpreted experiments under the old paradigm will be resistant to the new paradigm. These scientific allegiance to the old paradigm is

---

[36] Imre. Lakatos, "Science and Pseudoscience (transcript)," 4.

[37] Daniel Everett, Dark Matter of the Mind.

grounded in the belief that the truth of science is objective. Kuhn however argues that scientific truth is relative.

This implies that the notion that the truth of science is absolute is unfounded as Alston (1997) put it thus:

"But, of course, no amount of polemics against particular non-scientific ways to truth, however cogent each of them may be, suffices to establish the naturalist position."

What happens in Kuhn's view, is that, anytime the paradigm shifts, our stance under the old paradigm shifts into a fresh perspective under the new paradigm.

PART 11

THE CT CONVICTION MODEL OF THE DELIVERANCES OF
THE SPIRITUAL FACULTY

INTRODUCTION TO THE CT CONVICTION MODEL

I intend to critique, with regard to religious beliefs, the connections between *Pascal's wager*, Clifford's *The Ethics Of Belief*, William James' *The Will To Belief*, and Plantinga's *Warranted Christian belief*, in order to argue that the Christian theistic truth claims, in the light of biblical revelation and inspiration are epistemically justifiable from the Christian weltanschauung.

Other scholars including Richard Swinburne [38] and William Alston [39] have developed their own definitions of epistemic justification. The epistemic justification system that I advocate here, is one from the conservative Christian weltanschauung, based on biblical revelation of acquiring knowledge by the use of the spiritual sense or the sixth sense. This is consistent with the Christian doctrine of the spirit realm of the metaphysical or the sixth dimension. [40] It is, in the sixth dimension, that the deliverances of the spiritual faculty and inspiration take place. Hence, as my Christian theistic realism thesis, I shall argue that the Christian believer is epistemically justified in holding doxastic beliefs based on his / her persuasion of the biblical injunctions.

---

38. Richard Swinburne is an internalist about epistemic justification. As an evidential theist, he advocates a method of analysing individuals' attainment of religious beliefs involving the use of inductive criteria in probabilistic terms. (see, *Epistemic Justification* by Richard Swinburne Oxford University Press, 2001.

39. William Alston used to be an internalist about epistemic justification. In recent years he radically proposed a need to move beyond justification to an approach involving different dimensions of epistemic evaluation. (see *Beyond Justification: Dimensions of Epistemic Evaluation*, by William P. Alston. Ithaca and London, Cornell University Press, Ithaca and London, 2005.)

40. By the sixth sense, I mean, a dimension that is outside of the five senses, the sense experience that man uses to operate in the physical world. Plato in his 'Triad' calls it the world of idea' – the transcendental supernatural. William Alston calls this Christian Mystical Perceptual practice (CMP). Hence, the sixth sense belongs to the metaphysical realm, known to theistic Christians as the spiritual realm, where some agents participate in what Alston calls (Mystical perception), the Mystical Perceptual Practice (MP). William P. Alston, *Perceiving God: The Epistemology of Religious Experience* 1993 p.35-38.

My epistemic justification construct is predicated on the development of a 'Christian Theistic Conviction, which I coin 'The CT conviction model,' a positive epistemic status, which is a form of epistemic justification of doxastic beliefs based on biblical revelation and inspiration.

The central part of the CT conviction model is my concept of the 'deliverances of the 'spiritual faculty' as the 'hub' around which various segments of the model revolve for explanation, commencing from this introduction to the conclusion of the book.

As a preview of the coming attractions, it is suffice, to introduce here, the 'deliverances of the spiritual faculty' as a cognitive faculty, which relates to the process that forms our Christian doxastic beliefs.

A biblical text case of how a Christian theist, through the deliverances of the spiritual faculty operates the intellectual virtues of, for example, wisdom and understanding, is Exodus 35:30-35. The deliverances of the spiritual faculty shall be fully explored later as a 'reliable Christian doxastic beliefs forming faculty'.

Before I further elucidate my development of the 'Christian Theistic Conviction (CT) model, a review of the literature is in order at this juncture.

CHAPTER 7

THE CRITIQUE OF PASCAL, CLIFFORD, JAMES AND PLANTINGA ON THE GROUNDS OF THEIR PRUDENTIAL, EVIDENTIAL AND BASICALITY OF BELIEF FORMATION

While prudential, non-epistemic orientation for belief, for example *Pascal's wager* (1910); others including James' (1897) *'The Will To Believe'* and Plantinga's *'Warranted Christian Belief'* (2000) have made an immense contribution in this arena, there yet exists a gap with regards to an epistemic justification of Christian theistic truth claims in the light of biblical revelation and inspiration.

The apologetic ploy espoused by Pascal's wager is predicated on urging unbelievers, in the absence of compelling evidence for the existence of God to attempt to develop, faith in God on providential or beneficial grounds. That is, factoring costs and benefits into the analysis of rationality to construct a pascalian wager that God exists.

Pascal puts it thus in his *Pensées* (1910):

"Let us weigh the gain and the loss in wagering that God is. Let us estimate these two chances. If you gain, you gain all; 'if you lose, you lose nothing. Wager, then, without hesitation that He is."

The recent support for the Pascalian wagering by contemporary philosophers including Philip L Quinn, Thomas Morris and George Schlesinger is predicated on the prudential analysis of rationality for belief in God. There are of course, many formidable objections too.

Having weighed however, the support for and objections to Pascal' wager in the literature, I find the betting game deficient in leading unbeliever to genuine faith in God. To my mind the wager is gambling on God. This simply has the implication of inviting unbelievers to wager in order to avoid hell and gain heaven.

'Many God' objection is the one that I find most compelling. Ian Hacking and Richard Foley for example argued that the Pascalian wager,

"only considers whether one ought to believe roughly in the Christian god or not; consider how difficult it would be to use his method to decide which of all the religions that postulate a doctrine of eternal punishment one ought to accept." [41]

As the thrust of this work is to advocate for the authenticity of truth from the Christian theistic perspective, my argument is that the wager doesn't quite fit the bill. For instance, any theistic religion, say Islam can employ the Pascalian wager to persuade unbelievers to become Muslims, with a promise of paradise. As Diderot puts it thus,

'an imam could reason just as well this way' [42]

Pascal's motive is an attempt to convincingly persuade unbelievers that they ought to become Christians. It however doubtfully succeeds at this. Apparently we're aware from his Pensees that he intended to further develop his ideas more robustly but for his untimely death. Jordan [43] is right in asserting that the Pascalian wager only succeeds in depicting agnosticism and atheism to be irrational, leaving the question "which God?" unanswered.

Even if Pascal's wager, were to succeed in convincing an unbeliever to believe in a universal Deity, it would still leave the believer in a limbo as to which of the deities of rival religions to invest his trust? Should the new believer put his trust in a Hindu god, Christian, Jewish or Muslim's god? The Pascal's wager can't help him beyond this point. The apologetic appeal from a conservative Christian world view however, unequivocally will answer the aforementioned question in the affirmative – put your trust in Jesus, for "Jesus is the way, the truth and the life.... " [44]

---

41. *Gambling on God* edited by Jeff Jordan. Rowman & Littlefield, Reviewed by Kelly James Clark, Calvin College. Lanham, MD, 1994. p.2, available from Last Seminary, an academic resource for Christian research and education, http://www.lastseminary.com/philosophy-of-religion-article/ Internet; accessed 29 June 2011

42. Bernard Williams, 1981 – *Moral Luck: Philosophical papers* 1973-1980 p.98, Hacking, The Emergence of Probability (Cambridge: Cambridge University Press,1975), p. 66; see J. Jordan, *'The many-gods objection'*, in J. Jordan (ed.), *Gambling on God: Essays on Pascal's Wager* (Lanhan, MD: Rowman Littlefield, 1993), pp. 101–113

43. *Gambling on God*, reviewed by K J Clark, Calvin College p.4.

44. John 14:644. *Gambling on God*, reviewed by K J Clark, Calvin College p.3.

One wonders too, if prudential grounds advocated by Pascal are sufficient enough for authenticating the truth claims for Christianity, which is the focus of this work. As Kelly [45] pointed out "Pascal presented an argument about what is prudential to believe, not about what is true."

What I call the ethics of evidential belief is the driver, as I see it of the evidentialist's orientation to formation of belief, while the ethics of religious belief drive the conservative Christian theist's stance on formation of belief. The former finds expression in William K. Clifford's *The ethics of Belief* (1879), while the latter is a representation of James Williams' *'The Will to Belief'*. Clifford's popular dictum goes thus:

"It is wrong always, anywhere and for everyone, to believe anything upon insufficient evidence." [46]

Echoing David Hume (1748 Section X, Part I.) before him who said,

"A wise man . . . proportions his belief to the evidence,"

Clifford is forcefully asserting here, that it will be irresponsible for us to form a belief under any circumstance with insufficient evidence.

The story he uses to buttress his point is that of "a ship owner who embark on sailing his ship while in doubt as to his ship's seaworthiness. The ship sank leading to loss of lives."

Clifford hence produces a rational argumentation to the effect that

"the ship owner was responsible for the loss of life. Even, had the ship arrived safely, the ship owner nevertheless on ethical grounds would have been guilty, for his belief that the vessel was seaworthy."

William James in the *'The Will To Believe'* (1897), however unapologetically questions the principle underpinning Clifford's argumentation, submitting that in some circumstances beliefs held

---

45. *Gambling on God*, reviewed by K J Clark, Calvin College p.3.

46. W K. Clifford, (1877 [1999]), *"The ethics of belief"*, in T. Madigan, ed, The ethics of belief and other essays, Amherst, MA: Prometheus, 70–96

on prudential grounds are warranted. James argues that it is acceptable for our passion to help shape our beliefs, in circumstances where options confronting us cannot be decided on intellectual grounds.

James reasons that one goal of belief formation is avoidance of error. In this regard Clifford is right.

The second goal of belief formation however, is to belief the truth. Since Clifford's emphasis is that we must avoid error at all cost, James opines that to do so is to forever sit on the fence, that is to do nothing. In this regard we will never attain to the truth.

My miraculous experience, in the spring of 2011, while on holiday with my wife in a remote village of the pacific country of Switzerland buttresses the point. One day while returning from a trip from one of the cities back to this remote village, we arrived very late to the city train station to take us to the last train station where we needed to catch the only scheduled bus at 6.15 pm to our accommodation in the remote village. We didn't have a clue when the next train would arrive as no train time table was available at the station. The train didn't arrive until about 5.55pm. The Journey time to the last station where we must catch the last bus to the village is about 25 minutes. We needed a miracle. Either that the journey time be reduced, which only would be possible if the train was not delayed at any of the stations on route to the last station where we needed to catch the last bus; or that the last bus was delayed, if we were to arrive late to the last train station.

Now intellectualising in this situation was of no use. I did only what I knew was the only option. I believed that God would miraculously get us to the last station on time or that the last bus would be delayed. That was exactly what happened. We got off the train at exactly 6.15pm and the bus didn't take off until 6.23pm to the remote village.

According to Plantinga (2000), my belief has warrant as my cognitive faculties were functioning properly and were subject to no dysfunction in producing this belief, which was aimed at the truth of God's intervention.

James' thesis is stated in the *'The Will To Believe'* (1897), thus:

"The thesis I defend is, briefly stated, thus: Our passional nature not only lawfully may, but must, decide an option between propositions, whenever it is a genuine option that cannot by its nature be decided on intellectual grounds; for to say, under such circumstances, "Do not decide, but leave the question open," is itself a passional decision,—just like deciding yes or no,—and is attended with the same risk of losing the truth." [2-4, 11] [47]

James's thesis therefore permits formation of believe in the absence of proof or insufficient evidence, where we are confronted by 'a genuine option' which constitutes a choice amongst at least two hypotheses. A genuine option is where the option is 'live,' 'forced' and momentous. A 'live' option is an option of hypotheses that have an appeal to one's belief. A choice between becoming a `gay or never to marry is a dead option for me, whereas a choice between being an agnostic or a Christian is 'live, as I definitely will choose to be a Christian.

A 'forced' option is where taking an option is unavoidable between mutually exclusive hypotheses. As Pascal put it, 'you must wager'.

That is wagering for God is not an option, we are not free not to wager. We cannot, not wager. The decision not to decide is still a decision nevertheless, that is, suspending judgment when the evidence is inconclusive.

In the example of my trip above, I was faced with a forced option, I had to play, though the evidence was not available that I would get to my destination on time to catch the last bus to the remote village. I still opted to take the train. I exercised a belief, which was aimed at the truth of God's intervention. Yes, my belief, call it faith, delivered.

A 'momentous' Option as opposed to a 'trivial' option is where one option is unique and has a beneficial advantage over the other.

A J Burger interpreted James as simply saying

---

47. James William, (1897 Part 1). *The Will to Believe,"*

"Believe, if one wishes, by faith—that is, without evidence." [48]

James doesn't imply that faith is an action of believing in contradistinction to evidence, but that the will to believe is rationally justified, for example, when decision is made from 'a genuine option' with an inconclusive evidence. Part of this work is authentication of Christian theistic truth claims rooted in biblical revelation and inspiration. To this end, biblical definition of faith is

"the substance of things hoped for the evidence of things not seen." [49]

So faith is substantial and its evidence is grounded in believing. I once listened on TV to Steven Furtick speaking in a conference sharing how he spoke by faith to his church of 200 people in the first year of its inception that by the following Easter service the church would grow to 2000 people in membership. 2059 people showed up the following Easter service. Steven paraphrasing the aforementioned biblical definition of faith puts it thus "Our evidence of faith is our hope."

There is yet a weak link in the conclusion of James' defence of our right to hold a religious belief.

As my aforementioned argument about the Pascal wager's inability to sustain a genuine belief beyond prudential warrant, 'The Will To Believe' seems to be prone to permission of some kind of doxastic practices that are short of genuine belief that the Christian Theistic world view espouses. John Hick (1990:60) puts it thus:

"James's conclusion constitutes an unrestricted license for wishful thinking... If our aim is to believe what is true, and not necessarily what we like, James's universal permissiveness will not help us".

Critics have argued that 'The Will To Believe'

---

48. A J. Burger, "An examination of "The Will To Believe" in Ethics of Belief (1994 Part 1.)

49. Hebrew 11:1 (KJV).

"leads down a slippery slope to irrationalism." [50] James [51] has said that

"A live hypothesis is one which appeals as a real possibility to him to whom it is proposed."

It is this proposition that makes James's argument susceptible to religious belief abuse. Examples include the exercise of religious belief by unscrupulous religious believers such as David Koresh of Waco Texas who in 1993 led seventy-six Branch Davidians religious sect including himself and seventeen of the victims who were children under the age of 17 to their death. In a related incident on November 18, 1978, 918 Americans died in Peoples Temple sect led by Jim Jones, in Jonestown, Guyana. The dead included 303 children.

The gap between James's view and adequate epistemic justification of Christian theistic belief system, as I see it, is that, while James William in the 'The Will To Believe' tackles Clifford's criticism of irrationality levelled against theistic beliefs, he fails to deliver a credible enough defense that satisfies a Christian theistic world view. In line with my argument in the introduction, James's defense is deficient in providing an adequate justification for theistic truth claims. Again, as with the Pascalian Wager whose prudential warrant is most unlikely to produce in one, a genuine faith, which also falls prey to 'many God objection'; *'The Will To Believe'* equally comes under attack for its weakness in creating room for unscrupulous religious believers, to will to believe for ulterior, and often evil motives, as in the examples above.

Plantinga's *'Warranted Christian Belief,* though represents a giant leap towards rebutting evidentialists' objections, that the theistic beliefs are unjustified, unreasonable, that they are somehow intellectually or epistemically challenged, is nevertheless, a form of reformed epistemology that seems to me to be less rigorously defended conservatively. I am persuaded as do many other conservative Christians that the scale of Plantinga's argument tips

---

50. William James, Fideism - *The Will to Believe*. Standford encyclopeadia of philosophy. First published 6.5. 2005; substantive revision 9.9. 2009.

51. William James (1897 Part 1). "*The Will to Believe,*"

more in the direction of negative apologetics, an argument based on counteracting the atheistic, evidentialist stance or arguments that theistic beliefs are irrational at the expense of offering positive apologetics, that is, that the theistic Christian beliefs are true.

Plantinga (2000:10)'s work if anything goes as far as suggesting that the Christian belief is probably true and so only warranted if it is true thus:

"That is because (as I argue) if Christian belief is true, then it is also warranted;" [52]

The foundationalism and basicality of religious beliefs propounded by Plantinga, imply that any religious beliefs, whether pagan or Christian beliefs are true. This however begs the question as to which really is the authentic, true religion?

Throughout history, competing theories and views of truth abound amongst, theologians, philosophers and scientists. These world views include whether truth is subjective, relative, objective or absolute. The most relevant issue, however, for the purposes of this work, is a presentation of a case for biblical revelation and inspiration as a credible system of truth.

It is rife in the literature that, since knowledge entails truth-hood, knowledge is at least 'Justified True Belief.' (JTB)

Gettier type cases [53] are a blow to this assertion. In each of the original Gettier cases, a person justifiably believes proposition p,

---

52. Alvin Plantinga, (2000 xii preface), *Warranted Christian Belief*, Oxford: Oxford University Press.

53. In a typical academic controversy over role of justification in what does or doesn't constitute knowledge, B.J.C Madison refutes Sutton's argument (See Sutton, Jonathan. 2007. *Without Justification.* Cambridge, Mass.: The MIT Press. P.63-67) that, there is no distinction between epistemic justification and knowledge, that justification is synonymous to knowledge, since Gettier cases occur due to epistemic luck. Madison concludes that Sutton is implying that 'justified false beliefs' are impossible. Available from Madison, B. J. C. (2010). *Is justification knowledge? Journal of Philosophical Research, 35*, 173-192. Internet accessed on 27June 2012 University of Notre Dame ResearchOnline@N

but each of all the original Gettier cases involves an inference from a justified belief that is false. Hence Gettier claims that the person does not know p, i.e. has justified true belief that does not constitute knowledge. Plantinga (2000) however raised the bar of what constitutes knowledge with regard to the role of warrant in theistic belief. To Plantinga, warrant is what distinguishes knowledge from true belief.

Plantinga (2000:10) has argued that Christian theistic beliefs are warranted if they are formed by properly functioning cognitive faculties. Hence, if they are warranted, Christian beliefs are knowledge if they are true.

METHODS OF BELIEF-FORMATION ADOPTED BY PASCAL, CLIFFORD, JAMES AND PLANTINGA.

The above thinkers' methods of belief-formation can be summarized as follows.

Pascal in his wager rationally argues in the following propositional terms:

There is a providential or beneficial rationale to believe that p, if and only if (iff) p would guarantee that you win.

(P, is the belief that God is or exists.)

Clifford's evidentialist position

and

James's *Will To Believe* can be demonstrated pragmatically, in the example of my Swiss trip above.

I was faced with a forced option p.

I had to play.

I could not believe not –p. Though there was insufficient evidence for believing that p, getting to my destination, on time, to catch the last bus to the remote Swiss village.

In such scenarios, the evidentialist, such as Clifford's dictum [54] deontologically suggests, that it is my epistemic duty to withhold belief from p. I still opted to take the train, exercised a belief, which was aimed at the truth of God's intervention. Yes, my belief, call it faith, delivered. Internalists [55] including Roderick Chisholm and Lawrence Bonjour from the responsibilist conception of epistemic justification advocate the need for us to be deontological, that is, take our epistemic obligations seriously in forming our beliefs, if those beliefs are to be deemed justified. John Greco [56] put it thus:

"Thus we say that an action of S's is morally justified if and only if S's action does not involve the violation of some moral obligation. Substituting appropriately, we may say that a belief of S's is epistemically justified if and only if S's belief does not involve the violation of some epistemic obligation."

But in stark contrast to internalism, the externalists' thesis with regard to the concept of epistemic justification would be, that criteria other than performance of our moral or epistemic duties need to be explored. This is the driving force behind externalists' agenda including Plantinga's development of properly basic beliefs held in our noetic structures.

While Plantinga, in *Warranted Christian Belief,* is opposed to classical foundationalism's criteria for properly basic beliefs on

---

54. "It is wrong always, everywhere, and for anyone to believe anything on insufficient evidence."

W K. Clifford, (1877 [1999]), *"The ethics of belief",* in T. Madigan, ed, The ethics of belief and other essays, Amherst, MA: Prometheus, 70–96.
As noted above in James's response to Clifford, in *'The Will To Believe',* it begs the question, if justification of a belief can be based only on Clifford's straight-laced evidentialist stance. Will there not be occasions that warrant us to base a belief on insufficient evidence and justifiably so? This issue will be further elucidated later on in this work.

55. The form of internalist thesis here, consists in deontological form of justification, that is, the fulfilment of one's intellectual duties or obligations in believing that p, if one is to be justified in holding the belief that p.

56. John Greco, *Internalism And Epistemically Responsible Belief.* Synthese 85, 245-277 1990, 1990 Kluwer Academic Publishers. Printed in Netherlands P.246

evidential grounds, Plantinga himself is a foundationalist of sort. His concept of proper basicality for religious beliefs, arising from proper cognitive function leading us to have warrant for the beliefs that we hold, is grounded in Reidian foundationalism. [57] Hence,

"a belief has warrant for S only if that belief is produced in S by cognitive faculty functioning properly (subject to no cognitive dysfunctions) in a cognitive environment that is appropriate for S's kind of cognitive faculties, according to a design plan that is successfully aimed at truth." [58]

---

57. Reidian foundationalism refers to the epistemology of Thomas Reid, the Scottish philosopher, and a contemporary of David Hume, who having rejected classical foundatiolism, develops what is now known as Reidian foundationalism from which Plantinga in turn develops his warrant for beiefs.

58. Alvin Plantinga, (2000), *Warranted Christian Belief,* Oxford: Oxford University Press.p.15 While internalism on a deontological sense, demands that we must fulfil our moral and epistemic duties in order for our true belief to be justified or to be knowledge; Plantinga's externalist stance substituted, 'warrant' for 'justification'. So warrant becomes what a belief needs to have in addition to truth to be knowledge.

CHAPTER 8

DEVELOPMENT OF THE 'CHRISTIAN THEISTIC CONVICTION MODEL' OF DOXASTIC JUSTIFICATION

I argue below that the Christian believer is epistemically justified in holding a doxastic belief based on his / her persuasion of the biblical injunctions. The epistemic justification construct here, is predicated on my development of a 'Christian Theistic Conviction Model, ' a positive epistemic status, which is a form of epistemic justification of doxastic beliefs based on biblical revelation and inspiration. The Christian theistic conviction [59] model shall be hereafter referred to as 'the CT Conviction model'.

It's human to err. Admittedly therefore, as finite knowers, we are often mistaken in what we reckon to be knowledge. But can we as finite knowers know and can we know that we know?

To begin to develop my thesis of the CT conviction model of justification, it is useful to examine different sets of mindsets that exist in the realm of epistemology, with regard to how we know and how we know that we know. The conservative Christian theistic outlook to knowledge is predicated upon the premise, that the infinite personal God has created man to have knowledge of God and knowledge of God's purpose for man, though not exhaustively [60]. From this first premise we can move on to the opposing premise, that of presumption of scepticism. Scepticism presupposes the sceptic's thesis that includes a universal sceptic, that is, the sceptic who claims that we have zero knowledge about everything. There is of course, an inherent inconsistency with this claim. In other words, the claim is self-refuting, since we can argue that the sceptic's doubt, that we know nothing about everything reveals that he knows something about the subject matter. The sceptic has also

---

59.   The Christian theistic conviction here, is the conservative Christian's persuasion, a lifestyle in line with the injunctions grounded in the Biblical canon, the 66 books of the Bible declared as authoritative scripture by the early Church fathers. My main aim here, is to analyse the nature and function of truth from the conservative Christian's perspective and the credibility of biblical revelation and inspiration as a system of truth.

60. Deuteronomy 29:29, Romans 1:8-32

---

argued that, as finite knowers, we are often mistaken in what we claim to be knowledge. This raises the question, can we as finite knowers, know that we know?

There is a theory of knowledge called the KK thesis [61]. The KK thesis entails that if one knows, then one knows that he knows:

If Q knows that p, Q knows that he knows that p.

Roderick Chisholm modifies this thesis to become what he calls the Objectivity Principle:

"if a person knows a given proposition to be true, and if he also believes that he knows that proposition to be true, then he knows that he knows that proposition to be true. " [62] Hence,

If Q knows that p, and if he believes that he knows that p, then he knows that he knows that p.

What Chisholm is implying here, in his objective principle, a defense of his version of the KK thesis, is that, if p from an internalist stance is evident for Q, then Q knows that p is evident for him. Chisholm (1973) suggested that there are three world views that are involved in sorting true beliefs from false ones, in order to arrive at knowledge. Chisholm reformulated the problem of the criterion in terms of how two pairs of questions are answered:

"(A) What do we know? What is the extent of our knowledge? and

(B) How do we decide whether we know? What are the criteria of knowledge?" [63]

---

61. KK-thesis, i.e., the thesis that knowing implies knowing that one knows. Christopher Conn, "Chisholm, Internalism, and Knowing That One Knows". American Philosophical Quarterly, Vol. 38, No. 4 (Oct., 2001), p. 333

62. Roderick Chisholm, Theory of knowledge (Englewood Cliffs, N.J.: Prentice Hall) 1st ed. 1966, 2nd ed. 1977, 3rd ed. 1989.

63. Roderick Chisholm The Problem of the Criterion. Publisher Marquette University Press Milwaukee1973.p.12.]

The first worldview represents the sceptic's perspective. The sceptic reasons that: S can never know that p.

That is, the sceptic claims that we can never know the answer to (A) except we know the answer to (B), and that we can never know the answer to (B) except we know the answer to (A)

As I've stated above, the sceptic's response to the two pairs of questions is, we have zero knowledge about everything, period. The other two world views spring from what Chisholm calls the Methodists and the particularists.

The Methodists reason that:

For S to know any proposition p, S must have a criterion that answers the question how S knows, before knowing p.

That is, the Methodists believe that we know the answer to (B), and that we can therefore use (B) to work out the answer to (A).

The Particularists however reason that :

S assumes the stance of a knower, that S knows that p, without having to know how S knows that p.

That is, the particularists believe that we have prior knowledge of answer to (A) and that we can use our prior knowledge of (A) to work out the answer to (B).

The particularist's approach is consistent with the first premise of the CT Conviction model, that the conservative Christian theistic outlook to knowledge is predicated upon the premise, that the infinite personal God has created man to have knowledge of God and of God's purpose for man. Though man's knowledge of God is not exhaustive. That is, like the particularists, the CT Conviction model presupposes that man possesses 'innate knowledge' (see later discussion of Plato's triad in chapter 13).

Hence, S assumes the stance of a knower, that S knows that p, without exhaustively knowing how S knows that p.

Before I develop 'CT Conviction Model' any further, let's consider another aspect of knowledge – justification or beyond it.

Alston has suggested a revolutionary concept of evaluation of beliefs from a variety of epistemic points of view. An innovative epistemological approach to belief formation is Alston's *Epistemic Desiderata*. [64] This is the rejection of centrality of epistemic justification of belief. In its place, Alston proposed epistemic plural means (Desiderata) by which truth of beliefs can be established as clearly depicted by Alston (2005). Barnard Robert (2007) described Alston's epistemic desiderata as:

"a radical new approach to epistemology that rejected the centrality of epistemic justification, instead focusing upon the various ways in which beliefs might be good or bad from a variety of epistemic points of view, or relative to certain kinds of desiderata (or what he later called different 'dimensions of epistemic evaluation." [65]

Alston's advocacy for pluralistic approach to epistemic justification of beliefs, while rejecting the very idea of a single conception of epistemic justification encourages my venture into development of 'CT Conviction' model of epistemic justification of Christian doxastic beliefs.

Traditionally, in epistemology of belief, the justification of a belief is inferred from the property of that belief that converts the belief to knowledge. Then, prima facie, to answer the question how does a Christian theist know that what he believes is knowledge? I propose that a doxastic belief, and if further qualified, a Christian doxastic belief, is justified as knowledge, on revelation and inspiration of scriptures.

Hence,

(1) A person's Christian doxastic belief p is justified if and only if p is based on injunctions of scriptures. So,

---

64. William. Alston, (1993) *"Epistemic Desiderata."* Philosophy and Phenomenological Research 53: 527-551.

65. Robert Barnard, (2007) "Review of *"Beyond Justification*: Dimensions of Epistemic Evaluation"," Essays in Philosophy: Vol. 8: Iss. 2, Essays in Philosophy is a biannual journal published by Pacific University Library | ISSN 1526-0569 | http://commons.pacificu.edu/eip/ Internet; accessed 19 October 2012.

(2) S's Christian doxastic belief that p, is justified if and only if S's belief that p is based on injunctions of scriptures.

But recent development in epistemology of belief including virtue theory propounded by Linda Zagzebski has challenged the above 'knowledge inference from property of belief' type justification, as she reasons that,

"since justification is a property of a belief, it is very difficult to adjucate disputes over this concept if the belief is treated as the bottom-level object of evaluation" [66]

What Zagzebski, amongst other virtue epistemologists, is promoting, is a 'new normal' in the theory of knowledge, that knowledge, as tradition dictates, shouldn't only be inferred from justified true belief, that is, inferences from the property of a belief, but from the epistemic agent of belief, the intellectual virtue.

It will be interesting to see how the robustness of the 'CT Conviction' model Of the Christian Doxastic beliefs can be enhanced by incorporating the features of the Intellectual virtues of the epistemic agent, into the intrinsic belief's property (injunctions of scriptures) that confers justification on the Christian doxastic beliefs.

My attempt here, is to integrate the best of both worlds, in order to maximise better outcomes for epistemic evaluation of Christian doxastic beliefs. This approach is the distinguishing factor between an externalist's model say Plantinga's warrant and the 'CT conviction, a sort of an internalist's model,' since the Christian doxastic belief, in this respect, has a direct access to conditions that justifies it.

Christopher Jager articulates the difference thus:

"Warrant, in contrast to deontological and other forms of internal justification, is, primarily an externalist kind of positive epistemic status. It is externalist in the sense that the conditions which confer

66. Linda, Zagzebski. *Virtues of the Mind:* An Inquiry into the Nature of Virtue and the Ethical Foundations of Knowledge. Cambridge: Cambridge University Press. (1996, p. 2).

positive epistemic status on the belief are not directly accessible to the subject." [67]

What exactly are intellectual virtues? How can their deployment assist CT Conviction model in undertaking epistemic evaluation of Christian doxastic beliefs that are based on adequate grounds?

There are two schools of thoughts amongst virtue epistemologists as to the definition of intellectual virtues. The distinction is between cognition based virtues and character trait based virtues. The cognition based virtues are an expression of cognitive capability including accurate power of perception, intuition, memory and reasoning. These faculty based virtues spring from the externalist's perception of the world. The character traits based virtues, on the other hand have more leaning towards moral virtues, and internalist in orientation. They include what Greco describes as

'intellectual courage, intellectual honesty and fair mindedness'. [68] And on a deeper level also include bible- based virtues, understanding and wisdom, which are both intellectual and metaphysical achievements that are attainable by Christian theists and are far more richer than mere knowledge.

In the main, the character traits based virtues, are compatible with the objectives that the CT conviction model seeks to achieve in this work, on two scores.

First, in the CT Conviction model, the emphasis of investigation of what we know and the evaluation of how we know or how we know that we know what we know, the focus, is on the finite knower in his relationship with the personal infinite God who has made him a knowing agent, a communicating being.

---

67. Christopher. Jager, *Warrant, Defeaters, and the Epistemic Basis of Religious Belief.* Science and Religion, ed. Michael Parker and Thomas M. Schmidt Tübingen: Mohr Siebeck, 2004. P.6.b

68. John Greco, *"Virtue Epistemology"* in A Companion to Epistemology Second Edition edited by JONATHAN DANCY,ERNEST SOSA, and MATTHIAS STEUP A John Wiley & Sons, Ltd., Publication 2010. P.75

Second, in the CT Conviction model, the epistemic agent of belief, the intellectual virtues, are properties from which knowledge could be inferred.

Greco provided a representative view of virtue epistemologists' formal expression of what constitutes knowledge in terms of true belief as a function of intellectual virtue thus:

"In cases of knowledge, S has a true belief because S's belief is produced by intellectual virtue." [69]

In this vein, knowledge is defined as true belief grounded in intellectual virtue. To my mind, through the use of the CT Conviction model under construction, the whole of the human cognitive experience can be enriched, since the model advocates that, for Christian doxastic beliefs to be justified, they ought to be based on adequate grounds.

This is what virtuous Christians ought to do in line with the injunction of the scriptures. As Battal has remarked,

"Perhaps, what makes a belief justified is its being based on adequate grounds, and virtuous people routinely base their beliefs on adequate grounds." [70]

In the next chapter we shall explore how CT Conviction model can be used in the production of doxastic beliefs through a reliable process based on adequate grounds.

---

69. Ibid., p. 76

70. Heather Battal, "*What is Virtue Epistemology?*" Philosophy of Values Syracuse University http://www.bu.edu/wcp/Papers/Valu/ValuBatt.htm. Internet accessed 31 Oct 2012

CHAPTER 9

CT CONVICTION MODEL AS A SYSTEM OF EPISTEMIC DESIDERATUM

Alston's concept of epistemic desiderata allows us to hypothesize about evaluation of our beliefs from 'a variety of epistemic points of view.' In this sense the CT conviction model is an epistemic desideratum that shares similarity with Alston's preferred truth conducive epistemic desideratum. Possession of true beliefs is a paramount epistemic and cognitive goal within a truth conducive epistemic desideratum. CT conviction as a system of epistemic desideratum allows a fuller discussion of the nature and function of truth from the conservative Christian Weltanschauung.

As aforementioned, Pascal, James and Plantinga, have all cumulatively contributed to making the Christian theistic worldview credible. Our task here, however, is to answer the main research question thus: Are the Christian Theistic beliefs epistemically justified from the conservative Christian Weltanschauug, in the light of biblical revelation and inspiration?

We can now begin to fill the gap expressed in the introduction, as I see it, that exists in the prudential justification of religious beliefs employed by Pascal's wager and James' *Will To believe'* on one hand, and the generality that the application of Plantinga's warrant to religious beliefs entails, on the other. Alston provides a preferred explanation thus:

"Justification is an evaluative status; to be justified is to be in an evaluatively favourable position. For one to be epistemically justified in holding a belief, as opposed to prudentially or morally justified, is for it to be a good thing, from the epistemic point of view, for one to believe that p (then, under those conditions). We may think of the epistemic point of view as defined by the aim at maximising the number of one's true beliefs and minimising the number of one's false beliefs." [71]

---

71. William P. Alston, *Perceiving God: The Epistemology of Religious Experience.* Cornell University Press Ithaca, NY 1991.P.7

To fill the gap, I have proposed the Ct conviction model, in order to argue that the Christian theistic truth claims, in the light of biblical revelation and inspiration are epistemically justified from Christian weltanschauung. I shall argue that the Ct conviction model is skewed solely, towards justification of Christian religious doxastic beliefs.

Since the Ct conviction model claims the epistemic justification of the Christian doxastic beliefs based on biblical injunctions, it is little wonder, that the evaluative method chosen for this process is truth conducivity.

Truth conducivity suggests a strong tie between epistemic justification and truth, since the goal of believing is attaining truth. And the ultimate goal of Ct conviction model is to depict that we have knowledge by holding epistemically justified Christian doxastic beliefs, which are grounded in biblical injunctions. The components of knowledge being, belief, truth and justification, and as Becker [72] put it:

"of the three constituents *(belief, truth and justification)* of knowledge, only 'justification' is by itself an evaluative term, and it is also the only epistemic one."
(italics are my emphasis)

From the epistemic point of view, evaluating Christian doxastic beliefs as being epistemically justified and justification being a normative concept, implies we are making a normative judgement as to the rationality of grounding those beliefs on adequate grounds, [73] that is, on the biblical scriptural injunctions. Both Alston (1989) and Bonjour (1998) emphasize the need for epistemic justification to be truth conducive as follows:

---

72. K Becker, "" a peer review of Goldman's process Reliabilism. Internet *Reliabilism* Encyclopedia of Philosophy 2009 –a peer reviewed academic resource. www.iep.utm.edu/reliabil. . Internet accessed 29 Oct 2012.

73. I assume biblical scriptural injunctions on which Christian doxastic beliefs are based, within the CT Conviction model, as 'proper basing grounds' for Christian religious beliefs.

Laurence Bonjour:

Knowledge requires instead that the belief in question be justified or rational in a way that is internally connected to the defining goal of the cognitive enterprise, that is, that there be a reason that enhances, to an appropriate degree, the chances that the belief is true. Justification of this distinctive, truth-conducive sort will be here referred to as epistemic justification.[74]

William Alston,

"Beliefs can be evaluated in different ways. One may be more or less prudent, fortunate, or faithful in holding a certain belief. Epistemic justification is different from all that. Epistemic evaluation is undertaken from what we might call the "epistemic point of view". That point of view is defined by the aim at maximizing truth and minimizing falsity in a large body of beliefs. . . . Our central cognitive aim is to amass a large body of beliefs with a favourable truth falsity ratio. [75]

To explore the defining features of CT conviction model, we shall begin with what constitutes an epistemic justification for our beliefs. It is rife, in epistemology of belief, that a Doxastic and not a propositional justification constitutes knowledge for a belief. [76]

Let suppose that, two epistemic agents CT1 and CT2 are both summoned by Her Majesty jury service, as jurors on an armed

---

74. Laurence Bonjour, *In Defense of Pure Reason*, [New York: Cambridge University Press, 1998] p. 1.

75. William Alston, *"Concepts of Epistemic Justification"*, in *Epistemic Justification: Essays in the Theory of Knowledge,* [Cornell University Press: Ithaca NY, 1989], p. 83.

76. John Turri, aptly depicts how on basing relation, doxastic and not a propositional justification constitutes knowledge for our beliefs. John Turri *"On the relationship between propositional and doxastic justification*. Philosophy and Phenomenological Research, Volume 80, Issue 2, pages 312–326, March 2010. Epistemic basing relation as Adam Leite puts it, is the 'the relation between a belief and the reasons for which the person holds it.' in the article *'What the Basing Relation can Teach Us About the Theory of Justification'* by Adam Leite, Indiana University, Bloomington www.indiana.edu/~episteme/Abstracts/JustifyingAbstract.pdf. Internet accessed on 14 November 2012

---

robbery case involving J. On the prosecution's evidence for the case, presented to the jury, it becomes clear that J is guilty of armed robbery. Hence, formally in propositional terms:

G: J is guilty of armed robbery.

Both CTI and CT2 individually find J guilty of armed robbery. So CT1 and CT2 are each propositionally justified in respect of their individual decisions in believing that p.

That is, J is guilty of armed robbery, given the evidence of the prosecution.

On further probing CT1 and CT2 on their rationale for their decisions to believe that p, it comes to light, that CT1 arrives on her decision to believe that p, on the basis of how CT1 perceives J, that is, on J's unkempt appearance at the trial. CT2 however, bases her judgement that p, solely on the evidence given by the prosecution.

Given the outcome of this investigation, it's apparent that CT1, though propositionally justified in believing that p, is not doxastically justified that p, in the light of the 'epistemic basing relation' [77] CT2 is however both propositionally and doxastically justified in believing that p. That is, only CT2 is doxastically justified in believing that p, since she arrives at her believe that p, solely on the basis of the evidence of the case.

Formally,

P: J is guilty of armed robbery; q1 and q2, the reason/s for believing that p. Hence, CT1's belief that p is q1, but q1 is inadequate for justification that p, as q1 is a lousy reason for believing that p; whereas, CT2 's belief that p is q2 and q2 forms an adequate ground/s for belief that p as q is doxastically justified.

How one arrives at a belief often depends on one's normative's stance. For instance, holding a belief that p, for the reason/s q, as CT1 and CT2, each does, is an indication of one's normative position, which is equally driven by one's worldview.

For CT1, her belief that p, for the reason q1 is an indication of the assumptions underpinning her basing relation. In the case of CT2, however, her belief that p, for the reason q2 expresses her well founded evidence for her basing relation. In this sense, CT2's normative position q2, as an adequate ground, fortifies her belief, and so much so that she is not only propositionally justified but doxastically justified in believing that p, as well.

The distinction in this analogy, between CT1's assumptions and CT2's evidence, will explicate how only Christian religious beliefs that are based on adequate grounds – the biblical injunctions are epistemically justified, in a truth conducive sense, within the CT conviction model.

Being doxastically justified in believing that p, is also crucial for CT conviction model, with regards to the exercise of, for example, intellectual virtue of testimony' in acquiring knowledge. McDowell (1994), aptly expresses the need for an epistemic agents to be doxastically accountable, in order to have justification in attaining knowledge from the intellectual knowledge of testimony thus:

"---so that one can capture a knowers' justification – his knowledge constituting standing in the space of reasons – by saying that he has heard from so-and-so and that things are thus so and so.

We can protect the idea that acquiring knowledge by testimony is not a mindless reception of something which has nothing to do with rationality, but yields a standing in the space of reasons, by insisting that the knowledge is available to be picked up only by someone whose taking the speaker's word for it is not doxastically irresponsible… A person sufficiently responsible to count as having achieved epistemic standing from someone else's words need to be aware of how knowledge can be had from others, and rationally responsive to considerations whose relevance that awareness embodies. That requires him to form beliefs on the say-so of others in a way that is rationally shaped by an understanding of, among other things, the risks to which one subjects oneself in accepting what people say." [77]

---

77. John Mc Dowell (1994) Quoted from 'Knowledge by Hearsay', in Matilal, B. K., and Chakrabarti, A., eds, Knowing from Words, Kluwer, London. P.210-11

BRAINS-IN-VATS AND CARTESIAN EVIL DEMON

There is a mistaken assumption in the wider philosophical community, certainly in belief epistemology, in which a generalisation prevails, in classifying all religious beliefs as belonging under the 'brains-in-vat' or 'Cartesian evil demon' category. With such generalisation, it is easier to label all agents of religious beliefs as deluded, resulting in what is apparently an implausible conclusion that all religious beliefs are irrational - vices, rather than virtues, and so unjustified.

But are all agents of religious beliefs, brains-in-vats or deceived lots, by Cartesian evil demon? Two analogies depict the status quo in the academy. First, Putnam's (1981) analogy of being a brain-in-a-vat, [78] in this sense, implies that rather than an agent of religious belief actually experiencing what she claims to know firsthand, she is in actual sense, an isolated brain, packaged carefully in a science laboratory vat that feeds her brain with what she mistakenly believes to be factual sensory input. Second, the notion that the religious believer is deceived by Descartes' evil demon [79] and so her religious beliefs claims can only be taken with the pinch of salt, and then must be subjected to absolute verification process for certainty.

In the employment of the CT conviction model of doxastic religious beliefs, I disagree with this prevailing view and argue for the epistemic justification of the Christian doxastic beliefs.

To summarise, in the analysis of various component parts for the construction of the CT conviction model, so far, we know that, the model is a hypothesis of Christian theistic realism. We know that, the model is a reliable belief forming mechanism, that

---

78. Hilary. Putnam, *Reason, Truth And History*. Cambridge University Press, 1981 p.5. The Edinburgh Building, Cambridge CB2 2RU, UK http: //www.cup.cam.ac.uk. Internet accessed 29 Oct 2011.
79. Rene. Descartes, *Discourse on Method and Meditations on First Philosophy* 4th Edition 1998. Translated by Donald A. Cress. Hackett Publishing Company. Indianapolis Indiana.

differentiates propositional beliefs from doxastic beliefs, Christian doxastic beliefs being the justified beliefs that the model recognises. We equally know that, the model is a truth-conducive epistemic desideratum, in compliance with the truth goal of the believing enterprise. We also know that, the model invokes, belief forming processes used on higher level intellectual virtues of understanding and wisdom, in order to yield the desired output of wholesome knowledge.

In *"Epistemic Folkways and Scientific Epistemology,"* Goldman (1992) develops a different model from the CT conviction model. Goldman's model allows an epistemic evaluator to classify beliefs into justified, unjustified and non-justified depending on whether beliefs are generated by belief forming processes based on virtues, such as vision, hearing, memory and (good) reasoning, which have a high probability of producing true beliefs, or on processes based on vices, such as guessing, wishful thinking or ignoring contrary evidence, which have a low probability of producing true beliefs.

There are similarities of course, between CT conviction model and Goldman's model. They both allow epistemic evaluators to apply reliability test to classify beliefs into justified / unjustified dichotomy. The major difference between the two models however, is instructive, as it shows the extent of the divergence between the Christian theistic religious beliefs evaluation model e.g. CT conviction model, and the popular, traditional beliefs evaluation model evident in Goldman's model.

I suspect that, Goldman within his reliabilist account, will (if evaluated) lump religious beliefs with beliefs under the rubric of Cartesian evil demon induced beliefs and also what he called 'a class of putative faculties,'[80] that he evaluated as vices and so are classed unjustified. We cannot therefore, appeal to Goldman's model or any other traditional models, in arguing for epistemic justification of Christian theistic religious beliefs. Rather, by pursuing, in the CT conviction model, certain features of virtue epistemology from a different evaluative perspective, for example, what I termed higher

---

80. Alvin I. Goldman, *"Epistemic Folkways and Scientific Epistemology."* In Liaisons: Philosophy Meets the Cognitive and Social Sciences. Cambridge, Mass.: The MIT Press, 1992. pp. 99

level intellectual virtues, e.g., understanding and wisdom, is more consistent with the hypothesis of Christian theistic realism.

CHAPTER 10

THE NATURE OF DIVINE COMMUNICATION

The notion of divine communication presupposes the existence of a talking Personal Infinite God who has spoken to humanity. The Christian truth claims are predicated on the Christian beliefs (biblical injunctions) contained in the canonised books of the Bible, especially the gospel narratives. But how has God communicated to man? This leads us to the theological dispute as to whether revelation is propositional or non-propositional.

Within the CT conviction model, the notion of divine communication presupposes the existence of propositional revelation in which the Personal Infinite God has spoken to the finite man. In this regard, the theologian Matthias Scheeben's definition of revelation serves our purposes here. Scheeben having given an account of general revelation which consists in God's acts in creation in the natural world that is, non-propositional revelation], he moves on to define special revelation which is propositional in nature thus:
"In a more restricted and elevated sense, we speak of revelation as the act through which one mind presents to another mind the object of his own knowledge, and enables him, without seeing the object himself, to make the content of that knowledge his own, basing himself upon the lights of the one who reveals to him.... (M.J Scheeben, Handbuch der Katholischen Dogmatic (Freiburg, 1948), 1:10.)
    '...In still more restricted and more elevated sense, we speak of divine revelation as a manifestation through which God makes our knowledge in complete conformity with his own, such that we know him as he knows himself; this is vision face to face,' (Ibid.) [81]

HOW IS PROPOSITIONAL REVELATION EFFECTED?

This is another research question of my thesis, with regards to biblical revelation and inspiration as a credible system of truth.

---

[81] Quoted in John Lamont *Divine Faith*, Ashgate Publishing Limited England 2004. P.5.

The plausibility of propositional revelation is evident in the deliverances of special faculty in man, that of reasoning and communicative ability. Man is the only created entity who shares God's communicative attribute to perform intelligible speech produced from his thoughts. This means that the uncreated, Personal Infinite God and man, his created finite being, are talking entities.

Very much like his maker, man, has the communicative capacity to verbalise his thoughts in rational propositional terms.

Dawkins [82] fails to make a convincing argument with regards to a monkey's incapacity to produce on a computer keyboard, the Hamlet's short sentence:

'Methinks it is like a weasel,' compared to the ability of a 5 years old girl, to produce same sentence in seconds. The difference is instructive show casing man's self-reflective conscious state

---

[82] In *The Blind Watchmaker*, Dawkin's version of the infinite monkey theorem i.e. the typing monkey analogy, is to demonstrate via the weasel computer program, the difference between non-random cumulative selection, and random single-step selection. What is of much interest to us here, however, in the typing monkey analogy, is that, real monkeys, for lack of a theory of mind, cannot tell the difference between theirs' and others' emotions, beliefs and knowledge; And so are not able to turn 'thoughts into sensible sentences or propositions. So a monkey bashing away at random on a computer keyboard can only produce a gibberish random sequence of letters and symbols ad infinitum, let alone produce all the works of Shakespeare. Dawkins, Richard (1996) [1986]. The Blind Watchmaker. New York: W. W. Norton & Company, Inc. P.43

The following actual research report of behaviours of monkeys buttresses my point: "In 2003, lecturers and students from the University of Plymouth MediaLab Arts course used a £2,000 grant from the Arts Council to study the literary output of real monkeys. They left a computer keyboard in the enclosure of six Celebes Crested Macaques in Paignton Zoo in Devon in England for a month, with a radio link to broadcast the results on a website.

Not only did the monkeys produce nothing but five pages consisting largely of the letter S, the lead male began by bashing the keyboard with a stone, and the monkeys continued by urinating and defecating on it. Phillips said that the artist-funded project was primarily performance art, and they had learned "an awful lot" from it. He concluded that monkeys "are not random generators. They're more complex than that. ... They were quite interested in the screen, and they saw that when they typed a letter, something happened. There was a level of intention there." Quoted from the article: "*Infinite monkey theorem*", Wikipedia, the free encyclopedia, internet accessed on 3 Jan 2013.)

compared to a monkey's lack of a 'theory of mind.'

A lack of a 'theory of mind,' implies that, a monkey lacks mental states, which a human primate possesses (if he is not neurotypical, that is with no cognitive deficiency), for assigning beliefs, knowledge, desires, intents etc., to himself or others.

The possession of a 'theory of mind' also means a human primate understands that, others' intentions, desires and beliefs are different from his own.

The upshot of this is to show that man is the only part of our created universe that is capable of self-reflective, conscious, deductive thoughts that can be translated propositionally. Propositions originate from human thoughts, and can be translated into human language. Before I can utter the following in propositional terms, it is first consciously processed in thought-form thus:

'All birds have feathers'

The same self-reflective consciousness is in operation before I can produce a syllogistic logic in a form of deductive argument thus:

1. All birds have feathers

2. Eagles are birds,

3. Therefore, eagles have feathers.

In the same token, the syntactic language is exclusive to the humans who are endowed to use language recursively. This is the sense in which propositional revelation is the best fit for the CT conviction model. The model asserts that, as it is natural for all humans to make claims about truth telling, it is therefore plausible for Christians to assert Christian truth claims.

It is argued here that there is a correlation between man's in built capacity as a language user and the communicative Personal Infinite uncreated God who made man a language communicating being.

In this vein, Francis Schaeffer, [83] argues that through propositional revelation, propositional truth, regarding man's knowledge of science and also biblical historical account were communicated to man. The medium by which personal created beings received propositional revelation from the uncreated personal infinite being, is what Schaeffer [84] referred to as inspiration.

Hence, the following three levels support for the argument that the uncreated Personal God has engaged in 'divine speaking' [85] by 'propositional revelation' with the created personal beings are plausible thus:

First level support for, the argument for 'propositional revelation:'

1. While, all normal humans speak.

---

[83] "In such a case, there is no intrinsic reason why the uncreated Personal could communicate some vaguely true things, but could not communicate propositional truth concerning the world surrounding the created personal- for fun, let's call that science. Or why he could not communicate propositional truth to the created personal concerning the sequence that followed the uncreated Personal's making everything he made-let's call that history. There is no reason we could think of why he could not truly communicate these two types of propositional things. The communication would not be exhaustive, but could we think of any reason why it would not be true? The above is, of course, what the Bible claims for itself in regard to propositional revelation. Francis Schaeffer, *He is there and he is not silent*,. Tyndale House Publishers, Wheaton Illinois. 1972 p.82-83.

[84] If the uncreated Personal wished to give these communications through individual created personalities in such a way that they would write, in their own individual style, etc., the exact things the uncreated Personal wanted them to write in the areas of religious truth and things of the cosmos and history –then by this time it is pretty hard to make an absolute and say that he could not or would not. And this, of course, is the Bible's claim concerning inspiration. Francis Schaeffer He is there and he is not silent,. Tyndale House Publishers, Wheaton Illinois. 1972 p.83.

[85] Alluding to the plausibility of propositional revelation, Lamonts submits that the traditional Christian thought presupposes the existence of Divine speaking. That God has spoken to humanity. This implies that the Christian message originates from the existence of divine speech. John Lamont, *Divine Faith*, Ashgate Publishing Limited England 2004. p.5

2. No non human primate does.

3. Therefore, speaking a language, is a quintessential human feature.

Humans used to be distinguished from non-humans, in terms of humans, being users and inventors of tools. This emphasis has shifted somewhat. The measure of man's uniqueness as a language user is now rife. No level of investment into training of apes to get them to speak like humans or research into animal communication in general, has resulted in any evidence to match the high level of recursivity that is evident in human language or complex communication system of syntactic language in humans. Hence, given the truth of the first two premises, the conclusion necessarily follows the evidence, that, speaking a language is a uniquely human trait.

Second level support for, the argument for 'propositional revelation:'

1. Since man has a 'theory of mind.'

2. Man can self-reflect on the content of his and others' minds.

3. Therefore, man a language communicating being, can engage in a meaningful communication with other language communication beings.

As man possesses a theory of mind, and so is able to self-reflect on the content of his and others' minds, we can assert that we know, that, the only thing that can produce human language, that enables us to operate on the same wavelength as other people, is the human mind. It is a fair presupposition to hold that, the seat of human self-consciousness, (evolutionary scientists, admit the origin of self- consciousness remains deeply mysterious) on the Christian theistic perspective, is the human mind.
I equally argue here, that, the human mind, is designed by the uncreated personal God for the purposes of communicating propositional revelation to the created personal man. This logically follows the conclusion of the above stated, first level support that, speaking a language is a uniquely human trait.

Hence, given the truth of the first two premises, of the second level support, the conclusion necessarily follows the evidence, that, one language communicating being, can engage in a meaningful communication with other language communication beings.

Third level support for, the argument for 'propositional revelation:'

1. Man is a self-reflective, conscious being.

2. God, (the Mind behind human language) created man a language communicating being.

3. Therefore, man can know propositional truth by propositional revelation communicated to him by God (the Mind behind human language) a divine speaking being.

There is a consensus in the academy by both theistic and atheistic scientists, as stated by both Lennox and Dawkins[86] that 'the only thing, that we know can produce human language is the mind.

---

[86] In, 'Has Science Buried God,' a high profile debate organised on 11 Aug 2012 by Fixed Point Foundations at Oxford University, between Professor Richard Dawkins (evolutionary biologist) and Professor John Lennox (Mathematician and philosopher of science. The following dialogue ensued:

Lennox and Dawkins John Lennox: Let's go back to the origins of the universe and the origin of life. My life, as we both know has got this digital data base. It's got a language all of its own. Now, the only thing we know of, capable of producing language is mind. And yet you reject that. By definition, as an atheist you must reject that there is no mind behind this language.
Richard Dawkins: I do reject it. When you say, 'the only thing we know that can produce language', we know that what produces human languages is mind, yes we do, because that is human language......

Collins [87] demonstrated how the DNA sequencing of the gene called FOXP2 has a potential role for development of human language.

Hence, given the truth of the first two premises, the conclusion necessarily follows the evidence, that, man can know propositional truth by propositional revelation communicated to him by God (the Mind behind human language) a divine speaking being.

It is therefore the interaction of the divine mind with the human mind that results in production of propositional revelation.

As the nineteen-century theologian Matthias Scheeben aptly pointed out in the above quotation, first, in general terms, that revelation occurs when one mind presents the object of his knowledge to another mind with the view of imputing the content of the knowledge of the former mind to the latter mind. Then secondly, with specific reference to divine revelation, that divine revelation occurs

"as a manifestation through which God makes our knowledge in complete conformity with his own, such that we know him as he

---

[87] Medical Geneticist, Francis Collins headed the human genome project to successful completion in the year 2000, resulting into revelation of the information code carried within each cell of the human body. Collins reports on the implications for human language, of the discovery of the gene FOXP2, in his book 'The Language Of God.' A Scientist Presents Evidence for Belief.' Pocket Books, Simon & Schuster UK Ltd 2007, thus:

"The story of FOXP2 began with the identification of a single family in England where members of three generations had severe difficulty in speaking. They struggle to process words according to grammatical rules, to understand complex sentence structure, and to move the muscles of their mouths, faces, and voice boxes, to articulate certain sounds.

In a tour de force of genetic sleuthing, the affected family members were found to have a single letter of the DNA code misspelled in the FOXP2 gene on chromosome 7. The fact that single gene with a subtle misspelling could cause such profound language deficits, without other obvious consequences was quite surprising." P.139-140

knows himself; this is vision face to face," (Ibid.) [88]

The strength of the above three philosophical arguments for the CT Conviction model, proves that, for propositional revelation to take place, there need to be an interaction between the divine mind and the human mind. Hence formally,

S possesses R, iff D endows S with R.

i.e. S possesses propositional revelation iff Divine Mind chooses to endow S with propositional revelation. Divine Mind- God, chooses to communicate knowledge (propositional revelation) about the natural world (science), about history and the Divine Mind has chosen to reveal it through humans (Inspiration).

The naturalistic explanation of human consciousness arising from brain activities leaves more to be desired. This leaves us to posit the inference to the best explanation with regards to the origin of human consciousness. The plausible inference to the best explanation of there being a relationship between the human language and human consciousness is as demonstrated by my three philosophical arguments above; leading to the conclusion, of there being a relationship between the Divine consciousness /Mind and the human consciousness, which is consummated in there being propositional revelation communicated from the uncreated personal God to the personal created being.

Numerous researches have been carried out, such as I posit in this thesis, in support of how "theological knowledge, which though cannot often be proven empirically, howbeit, can contribute to epistemic maximization of truth. Corey [89] argues that the concept of supernatural agency is invaluable, as it can be profitable in building scientific theories and in final analysis, interpreting empirical data.

----

[88] Quoted in John Lamont *Divine Faith*, Ashgate Publishing Limited England 2004. P.5.

[89] Michael A. Corey, *Supernatural Agency and the Modern Scientific Method*, a paper presented at the Christian Scholarship: Knowledge, Reality, and Method Conference, held on October 9-11th (1997) at the University of Colorado at Boulder. Available from www.leaderu.com/aip/docs/corey.html. Internet; accessed 6 Jan, 2010.

Kemp [90] has also argued that while methodological naturalism presupposes a preferential appeal to natural causes over appeal to direct supernatural agency, naturalists cannot categorically substantiate their claims that the only way to gain knowledge is by scientific method. Collins [91] a distinguished physician-geneticist, once a staunch atheist, strongly refuted atheistic claim of genetic determinism, the notion that one's lifestyle is determined for one by one's genes. Collins argues that one's behaviour is largely determined by other factors, in the main, by choice – freewill rather than by biology.

---

[90] Kenneth W. Kemp, *"Scientific Method and Appeal to Supernatural Agency:* A Christian Case for Modest Methodological Naturalism." Available from http://www.stthomas.edu/cathstudies/logos/archives/volumes/3-2/kemp.pdf. Internet; accessed Feb 14, 2010

[91] Collins, whose accomplishments have been recognised by a number of awards and honours, including election to the Institute of Medicine , the National Academy of Sciences and a receipt in Nov. 5, 2007 of the Presidential Medal of Freedom, the USA's highest civil award, for his revolutionary contributions to genetic research; expressed this view at a joint meeting of the organizations of Christians in Science. Science and Christianity: Into the New Millenium Cambridge University, U.K. (2nd-5th August 1998).

CHAPTER 11

CT CONVICTION MODEL AS AN EXPLANATION FOR HUMAN CONSCIOUSNESS IN RELATION TO DIVINE CONSCIOUNESS VIA THE DELIVERANCES OF THE SPIRITUAL FACULTY

In his article, *"What is it like to be a bat?* ", Thomas Nagle's challenge, that, the philosophy of mind has failed to get to grips with the deeply mysterious problem of consciousness, still remains. He submits:

"Consciousness is what makes the mind-body problem really intractable "[92]

Michael Shermer [93] a sceptic, defines consciousness as "an emergent property of a billion firing neurons in particular patterns". Dennette's [94] (of the same school) main premise of his argument in his book *"Consciousness Explained"* is his claim that we can

"imagine how all that complicated slew of activity in the brains amounts to conscious experience... by thinking of our brain as information- processing systems, we can gradually dispel the log and pick our way across the great divide, discovering how it might be that our brain provides all the phenomenal."

---

[92]   Thomas Nagel, *"What is it like to be a bat?"* From The Philosophical Review LXXXIII, 4 (October 1974):435-50]http://organizations.utep.edu/portals/1475/nagel_bat.pdf

[93]   In a national science week debate held at Wesley centre Syndney Australia on "Does God Exist" between President of Skeptic Magazine Michael Schermer and John Lennox Oxford professor of Mathematics, and Philosopher of Science, published on the youtbe on 24 May 2012.

[94]   Daniel Dennett, *Consciousness Explained* Penguin Books Ltd 1993 p.434

There is no shred of evidence from neuroscience[95] to date, to confirm neither Shermer's nor Dennette's account from functionality of the human brain.

To complete the equation, we need to unravel as much as possible, (what Dawkins conceded in the aforementioned debate with the Archbishop Rowan William as "deeply mysterious"), the issue that lies at the heart of the existence of human consciousness. This issue cries out for explanation. As noted above, the naturalistic explanation of either genetic determinism or reductive explanation, that, the human consciousness arises from the activities of the brain (brain-states), is slippery and unsatisfactory, as alluded to by Bengtsson [96] in a reference to Jackson's [97] thought provoking

---

[95] In 2004, eight neuroscientists felt it was too soon for a definition. They wrote an apology in "Human Brain Function":

"We have no idea how consciousness emerges from the physical activity of the brain and we do not know whether consciousness can emerge from non-biological systems, such as computers... At this point the reader will expect to find a careful and precise definition of consciousness. You will be disappointed. Consciousness has not yet become a scientific term that can be defined in this way. Currently we all use the term *consciousness* in many different and often ambiguous ways. Precise definitions of different aspects of consciousness will emerge ... but to make precise definitions at this stage is premature."

Human Brain Function, by Richard Frackowiak and 7 other neuroscientists, page 269 in chapter 16 "*The Neural Correlates of Consciousness*" (consisting of 32 pages), published 2004. qouted in Wikipedia's article on consciousness. Internet accessed on 22 Jan 2013.

[96] "It has often been noted, and some have even based a substantive philosophical argument upon the fact that the content of our conscious experiences are not brain-states" David Bengtsson, in his article, '*The Nature Of Explanation In A Theory Of Consciousness*, p.2
Kungshuset, Lundagård 222 22 Lund. David.Bengtsson@fil.lu.se,

[97] Ibid.,
Bengtsson made reference to
Frank Jackson's article, "*Epiphenomenal Qualia*" 1982, and remarked on Jackson's contribution to the literature of the philosophy of mind thus:
"He there asked us what to make of the fact that even if we knew everything there was to know about what happened, when we experience a thing, in physical terms (in his case, colour), wouldn't there still be something left that we didn't know, namely what it was like to experience it? "

question on same.

Within the CT conviction model, we may posit, what a geneticist, Collins, [98] calls 'the language of God.' Hence; I argue [99] that, the human consciousness has encoded in it, the rubber stamp of the intelligent mind, the Personal uncreated being -God who has formed the personal created, self-conscious being - man, for the purposes of receiving propositional revelation.

There is a correlation between the divine mind and the human consciousness via the human DNA as a communication channel. Contrary to the naturalistic view, which is materialistic about existence, the Christian theistic view entails the account of the creation contained in the New Testament. This account describes the uncaused maximally great being as Logos, that is, the word, [100] by whom all things in the universe, the totality of all existing matter, energy, space and time are created.

----

[98] Dr Francis Collins when he was the Director of National Center for Human Genome Research, a cutting edge enterprise in the history of science, developed techniques to map genes that cause diseases such as cystic fibriosis. This project has charted the entire human genome. As a Christian scientist, he says, ' As a believer, I see DNA, the information molecule of all living things, as God's language, and the elegance and complexity of our own bodies and the rest of nature as a reflection of God's plan.') Source: www.cnn.com April 6, 2007

[99] The argument here is not a God of the gap postulation, but rather a pursuit of truth by rational analysis involving where available evidence leads us with regards to the understanding of the deeply mysterious issue of human consciousness.

For an example, the information contained in about 3.1 billion letters[consisting of four chemical letters] of DNA instruction book, cannot be explained satisfactorily on the naturalistic view, but rather points more to an intelligent origin, what Collins, (the medical geneticist, who led several other scientists in discovering the human genome, the DNA information code) called the language of

——[100] "In the beginning was the Word, and the Word was with God, and the Word was God. He was with God in the beginning. Through him all things were made; without him nothing was made that has been made. In him was life, and that life was the light of all mankind. John 1:1-4 NIV

So we may postulate of there being a possible world, [101] where, the DNA word structure is fed information by Logos – the word.

Here, I posit a possible world, a reality, in which the divine mind – God, designs human DNA information code, as a communication medium that is unique only to humans for receiving coded word – information, which can only be decoded by the human spirit via deliverances of the spiritual faculty. The apostle Paul puts it thus in Acts 17:28:

'For in him we live and move and have our being.' As some of your own poets have said, 'We are his offspring.'

Let's suppose this is what we call human consciousness – 'The infusing of the Divine Mind into the human mind.' This Infusing of the Divine Mind into the human mind, I submit, is the 'essence of the 'Divine Mind in the human mind.' This, on Christian theistic realism, arguably explains the foundation and the uniqueness of human consciousness.

Hence, from what we know about the human DNA as the information molecule, we can further postulate, that, the human consciousness is the immaterial part of the information, that is carried by the physical- the human brain. Ben Carson, a world class neurosurgeon in a panel discussion on science and faith with Richard Dawkins, Daniel Dennette and Francis Collins posits the divine mind as the source of the human consciousness thus:

"As a neurosurgeon I spent a lot of time dealing with the brain and the nervous system and I've been extraordinarily impressed by how complex it is. I'm also very much interested in human development and social development of individuals. And as a paediatric surgeon …and a lot of time dealing with children, and dealing with human potential, when I combine that with the scientific background, I tend to think that human beings are very different from other creatures.

---

[101] Philosophers use the notion of a possible world to explain the nature of reality. This lends support to the way things could have been, which is representative of the way things are in the actual world

And I think this is probably where I differentiate with some of my colleagues here on the panel who tend to think, it is all one continuum. However, when you look at the human brain and you look at what we are capable of, there is an extra sense of... what I call spirituality. Something that takes us beyond what an ape or a dog or a cat or a mouse is able to do, that makes us special, that makes us to be in charge of our environment." [102]

Further compelling evidence which supports my thesis within the CT conviction model, of account for the credibility of the deliverances of spiritual faculty, is made by Anthony Flew, the former world famous atheist, after his acknowledgement of there being a God. He remarked:
In his book, Conway attempts to defend what he describes as the

"classical conception of philosophy." That conception is "the view that the explanation of the world and its broad form is that it is the creation of a supreme omnipotent and omniscient intelligence, more commonly referred to as God, who created it in order to bring

---

[102] The panel discussion comprised of four distinguished thinkers -- Benjamin Carson, Francis Collins, Richard Dawkins and Daniel Dennett -- in a thought provocative discussion of "Science and Faith," recorded in Beverly Hills, California in 2006. The discussion is moderated by journalist Kathleen Matthews. Introduction to speakers is included on the You Tube video as follows:

Dr Benjamin Carson is a world famous paedriatic neurosurgeon who has performed revolutionary brain surgeries and is a Seventh-day Adventist christian. In 1987 he became the first surgeon to successfully separated Binder siamese twins joined at the head. At age 32, Benjamin Carson became Director of Pediatric Neurosurgery at Johns Hopkins Hospital in Baltimore.

Dr Francis Collins has among other achievement developed techniques to map genes that cause diseases such as cystic fibriosis. He is now Director of National Center for Human Genome Research, one of the largest undertakings in the history of science. This center has managed to chart the entire human genome. He is a scientist and a believer, and finds no conflict between those world views. (He says, ' As a believer, I see DNA, the information molecule of all living things, as God's language, and the elegance and complexity of our own bodies and the rest of nature as a reflection of God's plan.') Source: www.cnn.com April 6, 2007

Dr Daniel Dennett has confronted the philosophical problem of individual awareness, synthesizing advanced research in neurology, psychology, linguistics, computer science and artificial intelligence. He is a evolutionist.

Dr Richard Dawkins is now world famous as a foremost scientist in defense of the theory of evolution. He is a British scientist and author of the book The God Delusion.

---

into existence and sustain rational beings."[103]

Flew cited further evidence as follows:

In his book The Divine Lawmaker: Lectures on Induction, Laws of Nature and the Existence of God, Oxford philosopher John Foster contends that regularities in nature, however you describe them, can be best explained by a divine Mind. If you accept the fact that there are laws, then something must impose that regularity on the universe. What agent (or agents) brings this about? He contends that the theistic option is the only serious option as the source, so that "we shall be rationally warranted in concluding that it is God—the God of the theistic account—who creates the laws by imposing the regularities on the world as regularities." Even if you deny the existence of laws, he argues, "there is a strong case for explaining the regularities by appealing to the agency of God."[104]

Flew continued with more evidence:

Swinburne's central argument is that a personal God with the traditional properties best explains the operation of the laws of nature. Richard Dawkins has rejected this argument on the grounds that God is too complex a solution for explaining the universe and its laws. This strikes me as a bizarre thing to say about the concept of an omnipotent spiritual Being. What is complex about the idea of an omnipotent and omniscient Spirit, an idea so simple that it is understood by all the adherents of the three great monotheistic religions—Judaism, Christianity, and Islam? Commenting on Dawkins, Alvin Plantinga recently pointed out that, by Dawkins's own definition, God is simple—not complex—because God is a spirit, not a material object and hence does not have parts.

[103] Antony Flew; Varghese, Roy Abraham (2009-10-13). *There Is a God* (p. 94). Harper One. Kindle Edition.
[

[104] Antony Flew; Varghese, Roy Abraham (2009-10-13). *There Is a God* (p. 94). Harper One. Kindle Edition.

[105] Antony Flew; Varghese, Roy Abraham (2009-10-13). *There Is a God* (p. 94). Harper One. Kindle Edition.

Below, I produce a two-fold argument for the correlation of the human consciousness with the divine consciousness thus:

The first part of the argument:

1. The human DNA information code is uniquely designed by the Divine Mind as a communication channel.

2. Only the human DNA is uniquely designed with a high level self-conscious state.

3. Therefore, the DNA information can be adequately decoded by the human spirit via the deliverances of the spiritual faculty.

If what the former head of human genome project, Collins, the medical geneticist who holds that the DNA, is the information molecule, is anything to go by, and the fact that all rational beings hold that, humans are exceptionally unique, as highly self-conscious beings; also on the theistic view that man is a spirit being, endowed with deliverances of spiritual faculty, hence, given the truth of the first two premises, the conclusion necessarily follows the evidence.

The second part of the argument:

1. There is a possible world in which the Divine Mind - God in-fuses the human mind with divine consciousness.

2. Human beings are conscious in the actual world.

3. The in-fusing of the Divine consciousness into the human mind, as an inference to the best explanation is epistemically possible.

4. Therefore, the human consciousness originates from the Divine Consciousness.

Since it is a rational possibility, that a maximally great being, God exists in a possible world, then it is conceivable as an inference to the best explanation that ontologically, this greatest conceivable being is maximally excellent, and so capable of infusing his conscious essence into man, Gen 2:7 in order for man to be self-conscious in the actual world. Hence, given the truth of the first two premises, the conclusion necessarily follows the evidence.

Now let's consider a possible objection to the deliverances of spiritual faculty via CT Conviction model as an explanation for human consciousness and a plausible response.

The naturalist who is materialist about the DNA as the information molecule and about the divine origin of the human consciousness, may reject the conclusions to the above two fold argument for correlation of the human consciousness with the divine consciousness, on evolutionary grounds. However, arguments have been produced to the conclusion that the conjunction of naturalism with evolution are logically incoherent. Plantinga [106] posits that naturalistic view on evolutionary grounds is inconsistent. His argument is that, the conditional probability that our cognitive faculties are reliable in producing true beliefs will be very low if we hold the proposition of metaphysical naturalism, denying the existence of a being such as God of theism and the proposition that our cognitive faculties have arisen by means of evolution.

The logic behind Plantinga's argument here, is consistent with my CT model's explanation for divine origin of the human consciousness based on the deliverances of spiritual faculty. The improbability of possessing a reliable cognitive faculty on the conjunction of naturalism with evolution arises, for example, from the basic premise of evolutionary argument that, its primary objective is ensuring efficient functioning of the underlying neurology in a species, for production of adaptive behaviour for survival of the species and that if the underline neurology also produces belief content, it will be less preoccupied with producing true or false beliefs.

For example, a bat is endowed within its neuro-structure with an echolocation sense that enables it to sense objects by sonar, that

106. "*An Evolutionary Argument Against Naturalism* by Prof. Alvin Plantinga. The outline of the lecture Prof. Plantinga gave at BIOLA University.

CalvinCollegewww.calvin.edu/.../plantinga.../an_evolutionary_argument_against_. Internet accessed on 13 Jan 2013.

ensures its survival. Likewise, the human species are fired by their inherent neuro-structure to produce adaptive behaviour e.g. resulting in movement of their limbs for fitness and in search of food for survival.

Hence, with the conjunction of naturalism with evolution, even if the belief content of the intrinsic neurology fires our cognitive faculties to produce beliefs, it will be highly improbable that sufficient level of true beliefs will be produced. Hence, Plantinga claims that if we accept naturalism and evolution we have:

1. A defeater for the proposition that our cognitive faculties are reliable.

2. A defeater for any propositions that are produced by those cognitive faculties. That is, we have a reason to give such proposition up, a reason not to believe them.

3. A defeater for the conjunction of naturalism with evolution that they are self referentially incoherent or inconsistent. That we cannot therefore rationally accept the propositions.

Why is the CT conviction model via the deliverances of spiritual faculty' a default position for reliability of our cognitive faculty as an explanation for the human consciousness? The classical thought of St Thomas Aquinas provides an explanation

thus:

"Since human beings are said to be in the image of God in virtue of their having a nature that includes an intellect, such a nature is most in the image of God in virtue of being most able to imitate God (ST Ia

q. 93 a. 4);

and only in rational creatures is there found a likeness of God which counts as an image. . As far as a *likeness* of the divine nature is concerned, rational creatures seem somehow to attain a representation of [that] type in virtue of imitating God not only in this, that he is and lives, but especially in this, that he understands

(ST Ia Q.93 a.6)." [107]

It is plausible to respond to the naturalistic objection to the above two fold argument for divine origin of human consciousness by inferring from Aquinas' statement above, that, only rational creatures, humans have likeness and do imitate divine nature, God. On the Christian theistic view, this likeness of divine nature in man accounts for two phenomena:

First, the image of God in man, and this image as Plantinga has argued in his aforementioned lecture, implies that humans have reliable cognitive faculties to know things about themselves and the world.

Second, is in the first premise, that (the Divine Mind - God in-fuses the human mind with divine consciousness), amongst other two premises of the argument I have given above to the conclusion that, the human consciousness originates from the Divine Consciousness.

On the Christian theistic worldview therefore, since man is created a rational being in the image of God, which means, having a reliable cognitive faculties, man is capable of producing true beliefs.

THE NATURE OF GOD AND DIVINE REVELATION

Having so far explored the nature of man in terms of his self-conscious state and as a language communicating being, we require some knowledge of the nature of God as the divine communicator in order to understand what makes divine communication feasible. St Anselm of Canterbury's insightful work in 1078 provides an answer. Anselm's ontological argument is derived from his Proslogium thus:

"He is greater than can be conceived.

THEREFORE, O Lord, you are not only that than which a greater cannot be conceived, but you are a being greater than can be

---

107 .Quoted in "An Evolutionary Argument Against Naturalism by Prof. Alvin Plantinga. The outline of the lecture Prof. Plantinga gave at BIOLA University. Calvin Collegewww.calvin.edu/.../plantinga.../an_evolutionary_argument_against_ ... Internet accessed on 13 Jan

conceived. For, since it can be conceived that there is such a being, if you are not this very being, a greater than you can be conceived. But this is impossible." [108]

On an Anselmian conception of God, God is the greatest possible being who necessarily has the properties of being an Omnipotent (all powerful), Omniscient (all knowing) and entirely morally perfect being. On this conception of God as the 'maximally great being', we can postulate that all things have their existence in God including both contingent beings e.g. man and other necessary beings e.g. abstract objects, such as numbers, state of affairs, possible worlds, properties, propositions etc., and that abstract objects have dependent relation to God.

An antithesis to 'maximally great being' thesis, is the Omnipotence paradox, formulated to determine what is (or not) possible for an Omnipotent being to do. For an example, in his article, '*Paradox of the stone.*' Savage [109] proposes an argument to prove that the existence of an Omnipotent God is logically incoherent thus:

(1) Either God can create a stone which he cannot lift or God cannot create a stone which he cannot lift.

(2) If God can create a stone which he cannot lift, then he is not Omnipotent

(3) If God cannot create a stone which he cannot lift, then he is not Omnipotent.

Therefore

(4) God is not Omnipotent.

It is implied in Premise 2 that the Omnipotent being can

---

108. Anselm, (1033-1109): *Proslogium.* CHAPTER XV – "He is greater than can be conceived."Fordham University Of New York.
109. C Wade. Savage, *"The Paradox of the Stone."* In *The Philosophical Review*, Vol. 76, No. 1. (Jan., 1967), pp. 74-79

create a stone so heavy that even he 'cannot lift it.' This proposition is self referentially incoherent.

The phrase 'cannot lift' in premise 2, is meaningless, as it is incompatible with the very essence of an Omnipotent being. If God is Omnipotent he cannot be constrained or limited to the size of a stone he can create or the size of a stone he can lift.

Therefore the proposition is false, the reasoning behind it being logically fallacious.

The supposition in Premise 3 that an Omnipotent being cannot create a stone that he cannot lift is like asking God to create a square circle, make $3 + 4 = 9$ or make a married bachelor, all of which are logically impossible. As it is not in the nature of an Omnipotent being to do logically impossible things, this premise is also false. Given the falsity of premises 2 and 3, the conclusion does not necessary follow, therefore Salvage's argument is invalid

As demonstrated above with the invalidity of the 'Omnipotent paradox' argument, to the conclusion that God is necessarily Omnipotent. So by identical logic, God's Omnipotent property is identical with his Omniscient property.

If B is identical with C, C is also identical to B.

So, as for Omnipotence paradox, any Omniscience paradox or argument against God being Omniscient is by default also invalid. Hence, God is also a necessarily Omniscient being.

I stated above, that there are other nonconcrete necessary beings, that is, abstract objects. Contrary to platonic realism where abstract objects such as numbers are said to be independent of the mind, on the Judeo-Christian concept of God, we hold that these abstract objects, such as numbers, state of affairs, possible worlds, properties, propositions etc. are expressions of God's nature. St Augustine's view of forms informs our position here. Augustine [110] holds that the abstracta exist in the divine mind.

This point is crucial for the purpose of this section. That is, to

---

110. Augustine, *De diversis quaestionibus octoginta tribus*, 46.2. trans. David L. Mosher (Washington D. C.: The Catholic University of America Press), 80-81

understand what makes divine communication possible between the divine communicator and the human recipient of divine communication. For example, existence of propositions originates from God as divine thoughts, the means by which divine communication is instantiated.

Also an important task here, in discovering God's nature in relation to divine communication is the concept of divine simplicity which originates in Thomas Aquinas's classical philosophy. Aquinas claims that God is simple rather than complex. He is implying that God though, has a lot of characteristics, unlike man that he created, God is not composed of parts that include body, soul or matter and form of Augustinian platonic conception of reality. Aquinas puts this across succinctly in his Summa Theologica that

"because God is *infinitely simple*, God can only appear to the finite mind as infinitely complex." [111]

The strength of Aquinas' submission lends support to the concept of the deliverances of the spiritual faculty within the CT conviction model, whereby, God, who is not composed of parts, being an immaterial spirit infuses man's spirit with divine thoughts, that is, propositional revelation.

One more aspect of the divine nature requires exploration in order to explain the human personality in terms of its root in the personality of God. On the Christian theistic view, God is postulated as a personal being. Personhood defines the very essence of God to the very core of the constitution of the Triune Godhead, who expresses himself in three personalities, God the father, God the Son and God the Holy Spirit, and yet one God. The Apostles' Creed, as early as 390 AD affirms that the Christian faith is grounded in the three personalities of the Godhead thus:

1. I believe in God the Father, Almighty, Maker of heaven & earth:

---

111. Thomas Aquinas, *Summa Theologica I, Q. 3, A. 3 "On the Simplicity of God"*. Many editions. Quoted in an article "Divine Simplicity" in Wikipedia on line Encyclopedia. Internet accessed on 6 Feb 2013

2. And in Jesus Christ, his only begotten Son, our Lord:

3. Who was conceived by the Holy Ghost, born of the Virgin Mary:

4. Suffered under Pontius Pilate; was crucified, dead and buried: He descended into hell:

5. The third day he rose again from the dead:

6. He ascended into heaven, and sits at the right hand of God the Father Almighty:

7. From thence he shall come to judge the quick and the dead:

8. I believe in the Holy Ghost:

9. I believe in the holy Catholic church: the communion of saints:

10. The forgiveness of sins:

11. The resurrection of the body:

12. And the life everlasting. Amen. [112]

Swinburne [113] asks the question, what does it mean to be a person? He then introduces a concept of a person:

POWER

A person has power.

PURPOSES

A person has purposes.

112. *"English translation of the Apostles' Creed in the Catechism of the Catholic Church"*. Va. 1997-03-25. http://www.va/archive/catechism/p1s1c3a2.htm#credo. Retrieved 2011-05-19. Quoted in articled titled Apostle Creed in Wikipedia, the online Encyclopedia. Internet accessed on 7.2.2013. 113. In a focused interview with Robert Kuhn of Closer To Truth.com on the topic *"Is God a Person?"* Richard Swinburne the Emeritus Nolloth Professor of the Philosophy of the Christian Religion, University of Oxford, articulated his views on the personality of God in relation to man's personality as in the Christian theistic religion. YouTube video Published on 30 Aug 2012. Internet access on 23.12.2012.

BELIEFS

A person has beliefs.

From the above concept of a person, Swinburne contrasted the personality of theistic God with the personality of man thus:

God is a person as man is a person.

God like man has, power, purposes and beliefs but unlike man God is unlimited in these three aspects of personhood.

God has unlimited intentional power, while man has limited power.

God's purposes are free from irrational constraints, while man's purposes are subject to irrational influences.

God has beliefs about the world as man does. But man's beliefs are about only some issues of reality, not all issues of reality, some of which are true and some of which are false.

God's beliefs are unlimited about everything. That is, God has all true beliefs about everything, since he is Omniscient, he knows everything. Man's belief is a mixture of true and false beliefs.

From Swinsburne' analysis of similarities and the differences between the divine person and the human person, we can draw a conclusion as follows:
This triune God, is a personal uncreated being who has infused his essence into man to become a human personal being. [114]
I therefore submit in the light of the CT conviction model, that God is spirit, and in the main, is sufficiently detectable by the human spirit via the deliverances of the spiritual faculty. It is in this regard that I argue below that, the CT conviction model has a contribution to make in resolving the conundrum espoused by Alston in his Divine mystery thesis.

---

114. Genesis 2:7

DIVINE MYSTERY THESIS AND THE DELIVERANCES OF THE SPIRITUAL FACULTY

Alston's Divine Mystery thesis is that, the divine nature is incapable of being grasped by human positive concepts. He claims:

"no positive concept in the human repertoire (except for the minimum needed to secure a reference to God) can truly be applied to God as He is in himself. [115]

What I argue here, is that, admittedly, as deeply mysterious as divinity is, the non- applicability of human conception or cognition of God conundrum with regards to the description of who God is in himself, can at least, to some extent, (by no means exhaustively), be resolved, by our cognition being aided by the deliverances of the spiritual faculty. What Alston rightly referred to as "divine mystery" and without diminishing the seriousness of the divine mystery thesis, has already been given an explanation as aforementioned with reference to Deuteronomy 29:29 [116]

How has God revealed himself to my mankind? God is made manifest through Jesus Christ thus:

"In the past God spoke to our ancestors through the prophets at many times and in various ways, but in these last days he has spoken to us

---

115. William Alston, *Divine Mystery and Our Knowledge of God.* In the three lectures given by Alston (read by Nicholas Wolterstorff) at Yale Divinity School Convocation 2005 uploaded by Yale Divinity School www.youtube.com/watch?v=WOYib0Zm9W8 *internet accessed on 10.2.2013.Lecture* I: The Divine Mystery Thesis. Lecture II: Why We Should Take Divine Mystery Seriously, Lecture III: The need for true. One of Alston's conclusions divine mystery thesis. "That at the height of contemplative way the subject enjoys a union with God that involves God taking over one's life and consciousness and thereby sharing among other things, his own knowledge of himself as he is in himself, a knowledge that dispenses with the concept of any other representation.

116. Deuteronomy 29:29. Here, part of what God has revealed (again, not exhaustively) is how He would have us perceive him as He is in Himself. "For those things that are revealed (again, not all things are revealed) are ours or known to us.

by his Son, whom he appointed heir of all things, and through whom also he made the universe. The Son is the radiance of God's glory and the exact representation of his being, sustaining all things by his powerful word." [117]

Alston however, argues that the human cognitive power cannot truly grasp who God is. He further argues that even Jesus' divine utterances to man, eludes the grasp of the human intellect, since Jesus' utterances are expressed in human language.

This is precisely the point I have made so far in my development of the CT conviction model via the deliverances of the spiritual faculty, that man requires the sixth sense or spiritual faculty, as I have argued above, in order to receive propositional revelation (divine communication) from the divine mind. Alston quoting St John of the Cross confirms this thus:

"The only way to grasp God (*cognitively*) is to attain union with God in love which in turn requires detachment from all created things."

Italics are Nicholas Wolterstorff's emphasis. [118]

And Alston's conclusion:

"That at the height of contemplative way the subject enjoys a union with God that involves God taking over one's life and consciousness and thereby sharing among other things, his own
knowledge of himself as he is in himself, a knowledge that dispenses with the concept of any other representation." [119]

CLOSED AND OPEN SYSTEMS TO DIVINE REVELATION

The analogy that brings closer home the implications of the

---

117. Hebrews 1:1-3 NIV

118. Alston, Lecture II: *Why We Should Take Divine Mystery Seriously.* Yale Divinity School Convocation 2005. Italics are the emphasis made by Nicholas Wolterstorff who read Alston's three lectures

119. Alston, Lecture III: *The need for true.* Yale Divinity School Convocation 2005.

concept of closed and open systems, is the employment union closed shop system in Britain, before it was outlawed by legislation in 1992, in line with the European legislation. It used to be that people do not have access to employment in some industries, if, they were not members of unions within those industries. Employment could be said to be closed to such people for non-union membership reasons. For access to jobs in those industries you must have the union passport. After section 137(1)(a) of the Trade Union and Labour Relations (Consolidation) Act 1992 came into force, the closed shop system became an open shop system to which every Briton has an access.

In the same token, if we assume that, the ultimate reality is just matter and energy as naturalists hold, then, we are led to a system that is closed to the CT conviction model's deliverances of spiritual faculty, and in turn, we are closed to divine revelation. This is the sense in which the closed system is analogous of the divine nature that is incapable of being grasped by human concepts, on the Alstonian Divine mystery view.

If however, we accept as aforementioned, that the human consciousness (though deeply mysterious, as even the naturalistic, reductionist scientists conceded.), by inference to the best explanation, has a correlation with the Divine Mind – God, then we are rationally open to the CT conviction model's deliverances of spiritual faculty, and in turn, we are open to the process of divine revelation, to receive propositional revelation from the Divine mind. Formally,

S is denied d on the basis of n

i.e. S is denied Divine revelation on the basis of naturalistic perspective.

But;

S is allowed d iff S accesses d on the basis of sf

S is allowed Divine revelation if and only if S accesses Divine revelation on the bases of the deliverances of spiritual faculty.

THE HYPOTHESIS OF CHRISTIAN THEISTIC REALISM

With the CT conviction model, we are on to a radical epistemological endeavour of the hypothesis of Christian theistic realism.' I argue here, that the Christian true beliefs pass the test of epistemic justification for a Christian who holds Christian doxastic beliefs, when those beliefs are held on adequate grounds, [120] that is, on the biblical scriptural injunctions and that these justified truth beliefs are knowledge, as they are based on biblical inspiration and revelation.

Putting the hypothesis of justified religious beliefs into Christian theistic context, we are required to demonstrate how the integration of component inputs of truth-conducive-doxastic-beliefs through the employment of the CT conviction model, a reliable belief forming mechanism, can produce desired outputs of wholesome knowledge.

CHRISTIAN THEISTIC CONVICTION MODEL'S INPUT OUTPUT SYSTEM

INPUT		OUTPUT
Divine Mind via Propositional Revelation	Imparts	Knowledge to Human mind
Intellectual virtues, i.e. Spiritual Wisdom & Understanding.		Production of truth i.e.Christian Doxastic Beliefs.
The Essence of Divine Mind	Infuses	The Human mind with The Human Consciousness
Divine Speaking Being	Communicates	Propositional Truth By Propositional Revelation

---

120. I assume here, that the biblical scriptural injunctions are adequate grounds on the hypothesis of Christian theistic realism.

The test of reliability shall be based on the premise, that, a belief producing mechanism is reliable to the extent that, it enables a cognitive faculty to, for the most part produce true beliefs. From the analysis undertaken so far of the CT conviction model as an epistemic desideratum, and an evaluative process, it is demonstrable that, the deliverances of the spiritual faculty as a belief producing faculty, is consistent with this reliability criterion, since its goal as a believing enterprise is to produce true beliefs.

For this reliability criterion, we are postulating there being a possible world, on the Christian theistic view of reality called 'the spirit realm', for the schema S's belief that p at time t based on the biblical revelation (injunctions) is epistemically justified.

CHAPTER 12

CT CONVICTION MODEL AS A THEORY OF EPISTEMIC JUSTIFICATION

If we conceive epistemic justification phenomenally, as the connection loop between an epistemic agent (Christian's) belief to the truth, we can see how the account of the CT conviction model counts as a theory of epistemic justification.

By consolidating different segments of CT conviction model that have been developed so far, I now present the CT conviction model as a theory of epistemic justification of Christian true beliefs, postulating deliverances of the spiritual faculty as a belief producing faculty.

Before further analysis is undertaken of the CT conviction model as a theory of epistemic justification, it's expedient we examine similar theories of epistemic justification in the academy.

Swinsburne's division of justification into 'synchronic justification' (justification at a time) and 'diachronic justification' (synchronic justification based on adequate investigation) in his book 'Epistemic Justification' [121] is instructive as to the importance of clarifying a purpose for a new theory of justification amongst several theories on offer in epistemology of belief. Hence, the CT conviction model is a theory of the synchronic persuasion and of the kind that is unique and exclusive to the process that is capable of an explanation for epistemic justification of Christian doxastic beliefs,

In '*What is justified beliefs?*' Goldman extensively surveys various theories and finds almost none of them satisfactory on his reliabilist conception of justification of beliefs. My task here, is the critique of Goldman's method for evaluating justificational status of beliefs-forming processes in his survey, in contrast with the criteria for evaluating Christian doxastic belief forming mechanism, such as the CT conviction model.

---

121. Richard *Swinburne, Epistemic Justification.* Oxford University Press 2001.

The candidate theories that Goldman surveys include beliefs that are indubitable, self-evident, self-presenting etc., though in his article, he expresses these justificatory terms in a non-epistemic language, in order to serve his purpose of uncovering conditions that justify a belief. For example, Goldman represents a belief that is justified on indubitable grounds for the schema,

"If S believes that p at t, and p is indubitable for S (at t), then S's belief in p at t is Justified." [122]

Goldman's gripe is that, the status 'justified' is conferred on this belief without any causal explanation as to why this belief is held and sustained. He therefore argues that such an account of a theory of belief fails. The belief forming process is unreliable, because it is faulty. Therefore beliefs based on indubitable, self-evident, self-presenting etc., are unjustified. On Goldmanian view, the belief forming processes that are reliable have justification conferring status, in that they meet causal requirements for holding justified beliefs. The crucial point here for the discussion that follows, with regards to CT conviction model as a reliable Christian Doxastic beliefs forming process, is that, the Goldman's theory of justification is grounded in naturalistic epistemology [123] that looks to cognitive science to inform our understanding of which of our beliefs forming processes are reliable. We cannot carry out an evaluation of Christian doxastic beliefs on a naturalistic paradigm. We therefore cannot appeal to Goldman's reliabilist theory of justification for justification of Christian truth claims. This leads us toward the CT conviction model as a theory of epistemic justification.

---

122. A I. Goldman, *"What Is Justified Belief?"* in G. Pappas, ed. Justification and Knowledge (Dordrech: D. Reidel), 1979 1-23.

123. Goldman in the article below states his stance on Naturalistic Epistemologe (NE) thus:
"I shall continue to treat meta-epistemic naturalism as one type of NE, though we should recognize, that other, more restrictive senses of "naturalistic" are usually intended. These latter are best articulated not as meta-epistemic positions but rather as positions of one of the other two categories; a substansive position about knowledge, justification or rationality, or a methodological position about the way to study these topics." A I. GOLDMAN, (1994), *Naturalistic Epistemology and Reliabilism.* Midwest Studies In Philosophy, 19: 301–320.

BELIEF FORMATION AND THE DELIVERANCES OF THE SPIRITUAL FACULTY

The cognitive mechanism by which we form beliefs according to Thomas Reid [124] includes perception, memory, reasoning, testimony etc. Plantinga in 'Warranted Christian Beliefs,' asserted that Calvin's notion of Sensus Divinitatis is equally a cognitive faculty.

In this vein, I argue here, that the 'spiritual sense' is a cognitive faculty, call it, if you would, spiritual facility or spiritual ability or spiritual power. Origen, one of the church fathers alluded to there being what I call the deliverances of the spiritual faculty in contradistinction to what he calls 'a natural faculty' [125].

The 'spiritual sense or the 'sixth sense' is the Christian theistic view that a Christian agent (or a human person) is tripartite – spirit, soul and body [126]. The Christian theistic system, under CT conviction model, recognizes two intellectual virtue accounts. One account consists of cognitive faculties that include perception, memory, reasoning, testimony and so on, that operate in the Christian or a non-Christian agent's five senses. This aspect is sympathetic with the theory of justification of naturalistic epistemology that Goldman espouses.

----

124. Thomas Reid, Essays on the Intellectual Powers of Man, reprinted in Thomas Reid, The Works of Thomas Reid, William Hamilton, ed., 5th Ed. (Edinburgh: Maclachlan and Stewart, 1958), VI, v, 447.

125. Here Origen, in affirming the fulfilment of prophecies in Jesus, as a confirmatory reason for the Christian belief implies that, a spiritual faculty rather than 'a natural faculty' is required for operating a prophetic utterance thus:

"The proclamation of future events is a mark of a divinity, since they are not foretold by a natural faculty--- (Origen 1953:*Contra Celsum,* VI, 10, p. 324.
Quoted in John Lamont Divine Faith, Ashgate Publishing Limited England 2004. P.36
126. 1 Thessalonians 5:23 (New International Version):
'May Go himself, the God of peace, sanctify you through and through. May your whole spirit, soul and body be kept blameless at the coming of our Lord.'

Lamont's (2004) phraseology for this intellectual virtue account, is 'the deliverances of the senses can constitute knowledge'. [127]

The second intellectual virtue account consists of the 'spiritual faculty.' As a cognitive faculty, it relates to the process of acquiring knowledge by the use of spiritual sense or the sixth sense. This is consistent with the Christian doctrine of the spirit realm of the metaphysical or the sixth dimension. [128] It is, in the sixth dimension, that the deliverances of the spiritual faculty as a cognitive faculty, forms our Christian doxastic beliefs.
A biblical text case of how a theistic Christian through the deliverances of spiritual faculty operates the intellectual virtues of, for example, wisdom and understanding, is Exodus 35:30-35. [129]

---

127. Lamont distinguishes his intellectual virtue account from Thomas Aquina's account thus: 'I agree with those empiricist philosophers who claim that the deliverances of the senses can give us knowledge about the world, not just about how things seem to us to be. Aquinas denied that sense experience gives us knowledge of its objects. But I had that he is wrong about this. Of course we can think that we know things through sense experience, when we do not; just as we can think we understand a proposition to be self-evidently true when it is not. In neither case does the possibility of deception rule out knowledge where no deception exists' John Lamont Divicxne Faith , Ashgate Publishing Limited England 2004. P.133.

128. By the sixth sense, I mean, a dimension that is outside of the five senses, the sense experience) that we use to operate in the physical world. William Alston calls this (sense perception), sense-perceptual doxastic practice (SP).
Hence, the sixth sense belongs to the metaphysical realm, known to theistic Christians as the spiritual realm, where some agents participate in what Alston calls (Mystical perception), the Mystical Practice (MP). William P. Alston, *Perceiving God: The Epistemology of Religious Experience 1993 p.35-38*

129. Exodus 35:30-35New International Version (NIV): 'Then Moses said to the Israelites, "See, the Lord has chosen Bezalel son of Uri, the son of Hur, of the tribe of Judah, and he has filled him with the Spirit of God, with wisdom, with understanding, with knowledge and with all kinds of skills to make artistic designs for work in gold, silver and bronze, to cut and set stones, to work in wood and to engage in all kinds of artistic crafts. 34 And he has given both him and Oholiab son of Ahisamak, of the tribe of Dan, the ability to teach others. 35 He has filled them with skill to do all kinds of work as engravers, designers, embroiderers in blue, purple and scarlet yarn and fine linen, and weavers—all of them skilled workers and designers.

This is the sense in which the CT conviction model is a belief-forming mechanism via the intellectual virtues of wisdom and understanding. Here we have an account of experiences of two believers. First, Bezalel was filled with the Spirit of God. This triggered in him, the intellectual virtues of wisdom and understanding, which in turn triggered the natural artistic design skills. Bezalel and Oholia became artisans, skilled craft persons and much else besides.

PROBABILITY, JUSTIFIED BELIEFS AND KNOWLEDGE

Before further analysis is undertaken on reliability of the 'deliverances of the spiritual faculty' in producing justified Christian true beliefs, resulting in knowledge, it is crucial to consider the role of probability in arriving at justified beliefs, resulting in knowledge. As an operational researcher, I shall put my knowledge of probability to good use here. For example, in line with my claim for justification of the Christian doxastic beliefs, we may want to know how adequate the biblical injunctions as the grounds for a Christian theist's beliefs are, in making his beliefs probable. In other words, the adequacy of these grounds (biblical injunctions) are determined by the extent to which they make Christian theist's beliefs probable. Hence a Christian theist exercising choices in making a decision (p) in line with a biblical injunction amongst alternative decisions that are contrary to biblical injunctions, (-p) may belief that p as opposed to not p. For p to be justified it must have a probability greater than 0.5. The closer to 1 (certainty) the better as it raises the justificational status for p.

HISTOGRAPHICAL GROUNDS FOR CHRISTIAN THEISTIC BELIEFS

The Christian truth claims that I argue are epistemically justified, are rooted in the historical Jesus. Jesus's existence is upheld by virtually all the modern scholars of antiquity including biblical scholars and classical historians. The apostle's testimony about Christ's person, nature, death, resurrection etc., is contained in the gospels and the epistles. In fact the central theme of the whole of biblical scripture is about Jesus as the Messiah. This body of divine revelation is concealed in the Old Testament, revealed in the New Testament and constitutes the inspired biblical injunctions as a guide for daily godly living for Christian believers.

The body of divine revelation which includes the testimony of the apostles, constitutes grounds for Christian doxastic beliefs.
So, the sceptic may ask, are these grounds (biblical injunctions) adequate to make a Christian theist's belief probably true and so justified?

The position of the positivist or verificationist school, [130] from the deliverances of natural sciences (including Goldman's theory of justification) or the five senses, presupposes that knowledge gained from the spiritual faculty or the faculty of testimony for Christian beliefs is meaningless.
But I argue here, that a Christian theist, who bases her Christian doxastic beliefs on the deliverances of the spiritual faculty [131], call

---

130. Both logical positivism and verificationism are closely related, in that, their proponents (e.g. Karl Popper), believe, that theological statements or propositions relating to God are meaningless, as they claim, that, such propositions are empirically unverifiable, that is, by the deliverances of the five senses. For example during the positivist and verificationist era in 1930s and 1940s, to positivists / verificationists, propositions with reference to God such as " God created man in his image" or assertions such as " God loves me, for the bible tells me so" are meaningless and have no truth value. This view of course, no longer has any purchase in contemporary philosophy. For an example, Michael Polanyi's work was instrumental in exposing the fallacy of logical positivism - see Polanyi's book 'Personal Knowledge: Towards a Post-critical Philosophy.' 1958, Reprinted 1998, 2002 Routledge, 11 New Fetter Lane, London EC4P 4EE.
In contemporary philosophy, Theological propositions such as 'God exists', by principle of bivalence, is now widely accepted to have truth values. That is, it will either return true on the theistic worldview, or false on the atheistic worldview.

131. I find that, most theistic scholars who currently engage in debating atheistic scholars, shy away from expressing transcendental experience as 'spiritual.' For examples, Rowan William, then the archbishop of Church of England describes 'how Christian pray and understand their praying as what we rather unhealthily call spirituality' in his debate with Richard Dawkins (described as the world most famous atheist) at Oxford in February 23rd 2012, on the topic of 'The nature of human beings and the question of their ultimate origin.' I argue here, that there is such a thing on the theistic worldview, which in my phraseology is 'the deliverances of the spiritual faculty' that has a better purchase on rational explanation of reality from the Christian worldview

it spiritual facility or ability or power, induced by biblical revelation' from the epistemic point of view, is epistemically justified. In other words she is in her epistemic right in holding those beliefs and so has knowledge.

KNOWLEDGE BY TESTIMONY

As Matilal et al, in 'Knowledge by Hearsay' put it, that acquiring knowledge by testimony is not meant to be "a mindless reception of something which has nothing to do with rationality, but yields a standing in the space of reasons, by insisting that the knowledge is available to be picked up only by someone whose taking the speaker's word for it is not doxastically irresponsible..." [132]

The gap that exists between propositional justification and doxastic justification can only be bridged by being doxastically responsible. This doxastic responsibility with which a genuine Christian believer ought (and ought implies can, here) to hold his Christian doxastic beliefs, is key for handling the sceptic's doubt. If it can be demonstrated that genuine Christians are doxastically responsible, in line with what I call the acid test of non-mindlessness reception of testimony put forward Matilal et al, then the defeater posed by the positivist sceptic, that that knowledge gained from the faculty of testimony (for example, basing our beliefs on biblical scripture) is meaningless, is itself counterintuitive
The sceptic is mistaken in thinking that Christian theists, simply gullibly, Wily Neely accept any fairy tales around in the middle east of the first century, as the gospel truth. So we must answer the question, are the New Testament documents historically reliable? If the New Testament documents and in particular, if the gospels that claim to give true accounts of the historical Jesus are mere legend, then the thesis that knowledge can be gained from the spiritual faculty or the faculty of testimony for Christian beliefs is called into question. reliable? If the New Testament documents and in particular, if the gospels that claim to give true accounts of the

---

132. Matilal et al, in 'Knowledge by Hearsay', *Knowing from Words,* Kluwer, London. P.210-11.

historical Jesus are mere legend, then the thesis that knowledge can be gained from the spiritual faculty or the faculty of testimony for Christian beliefs is called into question.

The church fathers however, actually painstakingly with unparalleled devotion, use objective criteria to accept into the canon, authentic books, that are internally and externally consistent. The books meet acceptable, objective criteria for credible testimony that are historically reliable about the historical Jesus to confirm the truthfulness of the gospels.

The test of the historical reliability of the New Testament documents and the gospels in particular, includes the dating of the New Testament documents as generally agreed by New Testament scholars. The book of Acts was written between AD 60 and AD 65. The gospel of Luke which shares authorship with the book of Acts (the two books have similar literary style in terms of their grammar and vocabulary content), was likely to have been written between AD 55 and AD 59 according to the consensus amongst New Testament scholars. We know that the gospel of Matthew and the gospel of Mark were written prior to the gospel of Luke and so were dated between late AD 40 and AD 52. The epistles written by Apostle Paul, for example, books including Galatians and Timothy were written between AD 49 and AD 66.

We know that Paul networked with the church elders in Jerusalem, immediately after his conversion, having received a personal revelation of who Jesus is, as the Lord God. Paul consulted the church leaders in Jerusalem to check that his revelation of the Lordship of Jesus is consonant with theirs. So there was good communication amongst believers of the early church in terms of the agreement as to how Jesus is.

At the inception of the early church, Jesus was worshiped as God who divinely performed miracles. We know this is so by I Cor15:3-7's account [133] of Jesus' death, burial resurrection and appearances.

---

133. Bible scholars generally agree that, given the writing style of this passage in I Cor 15:3 -7, what Paul received was the belief of the early church after Jesus' crucifixion in AD 33, which was passed on to Paul by Jewish oral tradition which Paul in turn translated into Greek when he wrote 1 Corinthians in AD 55.

Paul reported that he received the information in I Cor15:3-7. The New Testament scholars agree that this information had existed in the Jewish Christian church within about two years after Jesus' crucifixion in about AD 33 and was a source of inspiration for worship of the risen Jesus as God. The information in 1 Cor15:3-7 was originally written in Aramaic in about AD 35 and in turn was translated into Greek when Paul wrote 1 Corinthians dated about AD 55. This information gives credence to the Jewish oral culture [134]

"For what I received I passed on to you as of first importance: that Christ died for our sins according to the Scriptures, that he was buried, that he was raised on the third day according to the Scriptures, and that he appeared to Cephas, and then to the Twelve. After that, he appeared to more than five hundred of the brothers and sisters at the same time, most of whom are still living, though some have fallen asleep. Then he appeared to James, then to all the apostles, and last of all he appeared to me also, as to one abnormally born." 1 Corinthians 15:3-7 NIV

as various ecumenical councils produced the biblical canon as a list of books that they considered to be authoritative scripture i.e. the books of the bible.

Dickson, the Australian ancient historian, in order to demonstrate why ancient historians including the secular ones take the gospels seriously, compares the dating of the New Testament documents that are similar to my above analysis of the dating of the gospels and the epistles with the dating recorded by Tacitus about secular ancient documents, for example, that of the Emperor Tiberius who reigned in the first century during the time of Jesus thus:

"The most important source for the life of Emperor Tiberius

---

134. The Jewish oral culture or tradition is one in which people memorise rabbinic teachings and relate them to subsequent generations. This is the mode in which the teachings of Jesus were preserved and disseminated. The disciples who became apostles received teachings from Christ during his ministry. This testimony is preserved via the oral culture which the apostle disseminated in written form as gospel stories. The church fathers used this means of preserving and transmitting historical events from generation to generation

(AD 14-37) is that of Tacitus written in AD 114 or 77 years after"
[135]

So the gospels were written within about 26 years after Jesus'
death. This makes the gospels the earlier ancient historical record of
the actual events of Jesus' ministry, death, resurrection and
ascension. This is far earlier than other secular historical documents
that we regard as reliable ancient documents. For example, our best
source about the life of Emperor Tiberius was not available for about
80 years after his death. This explains why there is a consensus
amongst ancient historians, about the gospels being the earlier and
most reliable historical documents of the first century.

We have demonstrated that the Christian theist is justified in
basing his Christian doxastic beliefs on the biblical injunctions. The
justification arises from there being an eyewitness testimony for the
accounts given, for example, in the gospels which enhances their
veracity, that is, the truthfulness and genuineness of the gospels. The
high quality eye witness testimony is as Apostle Paul puts it and we
have no reason to doubt his intention here:

"For we did not follow cleverly devised stories when we told you
about the coming of our Lord Jesus Christ in power, but we were
eyewitnesses of his majesty." 2 Peter 1:16

As aforementioned the gospels as historical documents
became available (within 26 years) very close to the actual events of
Jesus' life and ministry in the first century.

Therefore, being doxastically justified in believing that p, is
crucial for CT conviction model, with regards to the exercise of, for
example, the intellectual virtue of 'testimony' in acquiring
knowledge.

The sense in which we are justified in holding a variety of
our day to day beliefs on the information we acquire from
testimonies of others (scientists, weather forecasters, teachers and so

---

135. John Dickson, *'Why Historian Take The Gospel Seriously'*, a
presentation at Saddleback Church Lake Forrest California 2011 by Dr Dickson of
the Department of Ancient History, Macquarie University Sydney, Australia.

on) is parallel to the sense in which we belief the testimony of the old testament prophets in terms of messages they received from the divine source or the observations made by the apostles recorded in the gospels, about the person of Jesus, his nature, miracles, his death and resurrection; and of revelation knowledge received by biblical writers on various issues that are recorded in the Old and New Testaments.

Swinburne (2001) puts it thus:

"We learn to interpret what people are saying to us, on the prior assumption that people normally say what they believe to be true; and so, since, we assume, they usually have true beliefs about what they have perceived, that people usually say what is true. We learnt to understand what 'it is raining' means by hearing people say 'it is raining' when it is raining. And so generally. This is evidently the method by which investigators learn to interpret an entirely unknown language spoken by a newly discovered tribe. And plausible is the assumption in virtue of which we believe that we understand what speakers of our own language say now. But, if that is so, I could not discover by experience that others normally say what is true-because I have a belief about what they mean by their words only on the prior assumption that normally they are telling the truth. That assumption could not be established by empirical investigation...,"
[136]

PRODUCTION OF TRUE BELIEFS BY THE DELIVERANCES OF THE SPIRITUAL FACULTY

Now most epistemologists assert that, the trustworthiness of any of our cognitive faculties is mostly dependent on their delivery of true beliefs. In this sense, there is a correlation between reliability of our cognitive faculties and epistemic evaluation of our beliefs from the epistemic point of view. CT conviction model is an epistemic desideratum, that is, an evaluative system by which we judge our beliefs from an epistemic point of view. This means that Christian beliefs generated by this model are producing justified Christian true beliefs (jcb) in a 'large body of beliefs,' given they are based on

---

136. Richard Swinburne, *Epistemic Justification.* Oxford University Press 2001.p.124

biblical injunctions as adequate grounds (g). What is the truth falsity ratio? This kind of inquiry leads us to the maximal truths, minimal falsehood analysis.

Hence,

S's belief that p $\Rightarrow$ P(jcb/g) > 0.95

The probability of this state of affairs, that is, the probability of justified Christian true beliefs (jcb) in a 'large body of beliefs,' given they are based on biblical injunctions as adequate grounds (g), is expected to be very high within the margin of human error of 5%.

The 5% margin of human error here is not due to what Plantinga says, may be resulting from dysfunction of the cognitive faculty of the person who believes that p; but rather the 5% margin of human error is due to what Francis Schaefer says, that, man is made to know God not exhaustively,[137] but rather, as per what God chooses to reveal to man, Deuteronomy 29:29.

CT conviction model as an epistemic desideratum, an evaluative system, can only produce truth conducive beliefs (tcb) if and only if the grounds (g) (biblical injunctions) on which Christian doxastic beliefs are based are truth conducive (tc).

That is, if the grounds (g), (biblical injunctions) have propensity to produce mostly true beliefs (tb), as Alston puts it above, 'in a large body of beliefs.'

---

137. Francis Schaeffer He is there and he is not silent,. Tyndale House Publishers, Wheaton Illinois. 1972 p.83.

Deuteronomy 29:29 This is an important point, that, though, man can have knowledge, but he can only know what God in his infinite wisdom chooses to reveal to him. So the 5% margin of error implies, that, a Christian can sometimes be mistaken in what he believes. Hence, there is a need to therefore, make amends as he realises this, in an honest and open attitude that is a mark of a genuine seeker after the truth.

The probability formulation, S's belief that p $\Rightarrow$ P(JCb/g) > 0.95, implies the schema:

CT conviction model produces tcb, iff g are tc.

i.e. if g produce mostly tb.

Suppose we have X who believes in the following: a sense of direction via the operation of the 'intellectual virtue of understanding' based on the biblical injunction in Isaiah 30:31 thus:

"Whether you turn to the right or to the left, your ears will hear a voice behind you, saying, "This is the way; walk in it."

X via the deliverances of the spiritual faculty, the spiritual sense or the sixth sense, believes that she has God's leading to close a business deal that she has been praying to God about for direction. Is X justified in believing that p, i.e. that she hears God speaking to her spirit through God's Spirit?

Since Christians, for over 2000 years, believe in a possible world, in which via the deliverances of the spiritual faculty or the sixth sense, a Christian's spirit can receive divine communication via revealed biblical injunctions, as the adequate basing grounds for their beliefs, yes X is justified in believing that p, [138] that she hears

---

138. Swinburne arguing from religious experience asserted his principle of credulity thus: 'My conclusion about the considerable evidential force of religious experience depends on my Principle of Credulity that apparent perceptions ought to be taken at their face value in the absence of positive reason for challenge' Richard Swinburne *The Existence of God.* Oxford: Clarendon Press, 1979, p. 275.

Alston also having applied rigorous analysis to the experiences of subjects who claimed a perceptual experience of God concluded:

"The mode of consciousness involved is distinctively perceptual; it seems to the subject that something (identified by the subject as God) is directly presenting itself to his/her awareness as so-and-so...if God exists it is possible for at least some of these experiences to have that status." Alston, *Perceiving God: The Epistemology of Religious Experience. P.67*

God speaking to her spirit through God's Spirit. So she knows that p.
[139] Hence, we can assert, that, there is a 95% confidence level,
for a Christian, to produce mostly true beliefs, when she genuinely
bases her Christian doxastic beliefs on adequate grounds of the
divinely revealed biblical injunctions. But how do we account for the
5% margin of human error? Could we sometimes be mistaken in our
belief, that we receive a divine communication on the basis of
biblical injunction? As it is human to err, yes, and a genuine
Christian will be the first to admit that she could sometimes be
mistaken, and be prepared to make any necessary amends.

But how do we guide against foolhardiness when we make
Christian truth claims? There are some people who claim to be
Christians (cognitive dysfunction apart) and that they receive divine
revelation to do what is unscriptural and so irrationally put God to
the test.

For example, a few years ago, a Londoner claimed that, in the name
of God, he was sent to jump from the London zoo security fence into
the lion cage at the London zoo.
He became an easy pray for the wild beast as he was brutally
attacked by the Lion.
It goes without saying, that in this case, the Londoner's belief did not
have any justificational status, as what he did was unscriptural, that
is, his belief was not based on any biblical injunctions and so not

---

139 X here, can claim to have knowledge like S does in her experience of God, in
Alston's documented experience of a Christian believer who is referred to as (1) in
the quotation below: To be sure, in using a comparative concept of looks like a P
to characterize an experience, S is assuming that he knows what a P looks like (in
normal conditions or whatever), and this assumption may be challenged. How
does (1) know how a supremely good or powerful being would present itself to his
experience? The obvious answer is that it is the person's experience with more
humble exemplifications of these features that puts him/her in this position. If one
has been involved in relationships with other human beings, one knows what it is
like to be aware of another person's expressing his love for one. One's experience
with more or less good human beings has presumably given (1) some idea as to
what it is like, experientially, to be interacting with a good person manifesting his
goodness, as contrasted with what it is like experientially to be interacting with an
evil person manifesting that quality. And so on. This enables the subject to use
these comparative terms to conceptualize a certain mode of divine appearance."
Alston, *Perceiving God: The Epistemology of Religious Experience. P.47-48.*

based on adequate grounds.

Such inanity apart, a genuine Christian who sincerely submits to the leading of God's Spirit, as a is a tripartite being and essentially a spirit, can receive divine communication.

CHAPTER 13

CT CONVICTION MODEL THESIS (VIEW OF REALITY)

In this last chapter I shall pull together different threads of the CT Conviction model in order to draw a conclusion based on the CT Conviction view of reality. To this end, I shall adopt a Hegelian dialectical triad of thesis, antithesis and synthesis as follows.

HEGELIAN DIALECTICAL TRIAD METHODOLOGICAL APPROACH:

Adopting Hegelian dialectic, we can rationally suppose that humans desire to know the whole truth, hence the role of rational argumentation in processing alternating arguments. In virtue of rational argumentation, every argument attracts a counter argument. Hence, I call the original argument, the thesis. The thesis as a single idea in this sense is incomplete and therefore gives rise to a counter argument, that is, the antithesis arising from the conflict that the thesis generates. To resolve the conflict therefore, we need to reconcile the truths that are contained in the thesis and antithesis at a new higher dimension to form a synthesis, the whole truth.

From prior analysis undertaken within the CT Conviction model so far, we have:

THE THESIS:

From the Christian theistic worldview, the 'deliverances of the spiritual faculty' as a cognitive faculty, is the process of acquiring knowledge of Christian doxastic true beliefs by employing spiritual sense or the sixth sense. This is the doctrine of the spirit realm of the metaphysical or the sixth dimension. It is, in the sixth dimension (the spiritual dimension), that the deliverances of the spiritual faculty as a cognitive faculty, forms our Christian doxastic beliefs.

THE ANTITHESIS:

From the position of the positivist, verificationist or naturalist world view, the deliverances of natural sciences or the five senses, presuppose that knowledge gained from the spiritual faculty or the faculty of testimony for Christian beliefs is meaningless.

THE SYNTHESIS:

Before we arrive at the synthesis, we need to cover more grounds. We shall commence with the war of worldviews that the above stated thesis and antithesis are engaged in.

THE WAR OF WORLDVIEWS

In the pre modern era, the period from the middle ages to 1600, the human society moves from a 'God centred truth' reality to now a bifurcation of nature (scientific) truth and religious truth. The 'truth goal' of this work, is to argue that, from God's standpoint established in scriptural injunctions, that there is no division between nature (science) / religious truth of reality. There is really only one reality – the objective truth, which was the status quote before the Enlightenment in the 17th Century. The main distinction therefore, between the thesis and the 'antithesis' of my Hegelian triad construct is predicated on one's perspective of truth that entails one's perspective of reality. The Ct Conviction model for Christian truth claims that are grounded in injunction of scriptures, is a theological hypothesis, which, if true, would make such theistic beliefs, a form of knowledge. (Thesis.)

The Ct conviction model operates in the realm of the metaphysical. Reasoning metaphysically, we often ask; why does earthquake kill people and destroy property?

Is there life after death? Why do bad things happen to good people? These and similar questions are expressions of humankind's desire for answers to life's intricate questions predicated on their quest to understand the nature of reality in their world.

The answers that one gets to these questions are indicators of diverse conceptions of reality. Two schools of thought often emerge from the answers: People who have a teleological conception of reality on one hand, ground their belief in certain causes, as triggers for the reality as they perceive it. The theistic school falls into this category. (Thesis.)

On the other hand, there is a naturalistic conception of reality, grounded in scientific causation. The naturalistic school falls into this category. (Antithesis) To the naturalistic school, the aforementioned questions are scientifically determined, that is, the naturalists' reality is coloured by scientific objectivity – the nomological explanation of reality. Hence, the cause of the earthquake or Tsunami that strikes to destroy a community of people is only investigated scientifically with no strings attached.

To the theistic school however, reality is also transcendental. The transcendence here is a scope of reality that reflects the realm of the universals as opposed to just the existence of particulars on the naturalistic view of reality. That is, metaphysical thinking with regards to the ultimate nature of reality that entails intelligence and purpose – the axiological explanation of reality.

Ward contrasts nomological explanation with axiological explanation to differentiate an explanation that is a best fit for scientific / materialistic view of reality from an explanation for a valued base, immaterial, transcendental view of reality thus: "Nomological explanation, is a scientific explanation which refers to laws, e.g. if A then B and describes what happens, It does not make reference to the future. It just says here is the law, you just need an initial conditions and the law, then you can perhaps predict....Axiological explanation is an explanation in terms of reasons for the sake of which you will do an action... I'm doing some action (something) in order to bring about some effect which I think it is good." [140]

Ward's above definitions inform our understanding of which of the explanations of the universe best describes on one hand the above 'thesis' and the other hand the 'antithesis.' Obviously, the above 'thesis' is best represented by the axiological explanation while the 'nomological' explanation, is a best fit for the' antithesis.' Any attempt at nomological explanation to negate the 'thesis' that, only the deliverances of the spiritual faculty produces knowledge of our Christian doxastic true beliefs, will simply lead us to logical

---

140. Keith Ward, a philosopher and the former regent professorship of divinity at Oxford University, in debate with Aris Hamed, a Cambridge University philosopher and on *"The Christian & Athiest philosophers' worldviews* organised by Veritas.org in Cambridge University in January 2013.

meaninglessness. The reason being that scientism (the notion that only the scientific explanation counts) or materialism rigidly presupposes that, all there is, (even thoughts, mind, consciousness and so on) essentially emerges from matter. So the materialist's argument goes, say with regards to the existence of God thus:

1. All that exists is material.

2. By nature God is immaterial.

3. Therefore, God doesn't exist.

The fallacy of the above argument based on the deductive-nomological explanation is crystal clear. It simply demonstrates the limits of science or methodological naturalism in providing explanation for issues that lie outside the competence of science. Given the falsity of the first premise, the conclusion does not follow the evidence, hence the argument fails as it is invalid.

Applying the principles of formal axiology as stated below, by Hartman the father of modern axiology, to the above argument in value terms, produces a new but rational argumentation:

"Formal axiology.... does organically relate signification (intention) and significance (value); it does so systematically and with precision. They are combined by the value of axiom, The value of the thing is the fulfilment of its intension. The meaning of a thing in terms of its value is the fulfilment of its logical meaning. The axiological meaning of a thing is fulfilment of its logical meaning." [141]

So the idealist's argument goes, say with regards to the existence of God thus:

1. The whole of meaningful existence consists of both the material and the immaterial.

2. The transcendental objective, purposeful, immaterial God

---

141. Robert S. Hartman, *The Knowledge of Good: Critique of Axiological Reason* (Value Inquiry Book) 2002 Chapter 10: Synthetic Value Measurement and Prediction p.325.

created the universe of the material and immaterial composition.

2. The transcendental objective, purposeful, immaterial God created the universe of the material and immaterial composition.

3. Therefore, the meaningful, purposeful God exists.

Given the truth of the two premises, the conclusion does follow the evidence.

Hence, axiologiucally, the value of God's purpose is fulfilled in meaningful creation of the universe of the material and immaterial composition, leading to there being an intelligent mind, God, behind the purposeful and meaningful universe.

THE ANTITHESIS: NOMOLOGICAL EXPLANATION – A DISCOURSE

The failure of the materialist's argument against the existence of God, calls for an in-depth discourse of the antithesis and its grounding in naturalistic worldview.

From the materialist conception of truth or existence, it becomes a necessary truth that everything that exists must exist in somewhat, material form. So contrary to the arguments I have produced above, leading to the thesis, for example, on the divine origin of consciousness, the antithesis, from the materialist' worldview construes, the mental states - any associated properties of consciousness e.g., mind, mental thoughts, feelings as causally dependent on the material brain states.

Another worldview that is a ground for the antithesis' nomological position is empiricism. This is the view that grounds beliefs on observational evidence. In this regard the antithesis is that we cannot claim to have knowledge without empirical proof for our beliefs. This worldview is again predicated on there being no existence beyond matter – the material universe in contrast to the transcendental existence. To the empiricist therefore, what we can know is limited to our experience of the material universe. There is a correlation between empiricist' worldview and the naturalist conception of reality which entails materialism. For example, to the quantum physicist, reality may be reducible to a wave function in some multidimensional space. It is little wonder then that an empiricist may fail to appreciate the validity of the theistic argument regarding holding beliefs produced by deliverances of the spiritual faculty that the thesis upholds.

THE THESIS: AXIOLOGICAL EXPLANATION – A DISCOURSE

Idealistically, the grounds for the claim in the above thesis follows an axiological explanation that is not reducible to nomological or scientific explanation.

The thesis, that, we acquire knowledge of Christian doxastic true beliefs via the 'deliverances of the spiritual faculty' presupposes, in contradistinction to the worldview in the antithesis, that, there is more than the existence of matter. The deliverances of spiritual faculty are also predicated on the human consciousness being irreducible to material brain states. Hence, consciousness is real as already noted above in the rational argumentation I made about the divine origin of human consciousness.

As the thesis implies that there is more than matter in the universe, it is an intelligible supposition, that there is correlation between human consciousness and the physical world.

That is, there is a relationship between the physical (the material) and the human consciousness- the continuing substantial self, which in theology is called the soul (the spiritual- because a man's spirit is an immaterial part of his soul (essence) especially for contact with the Divine spirit, God).

The reality of consciousness leads us to the notion of consciousness as un-embodied mind. Descartes, in meditation six [142] is right in distinguishing between the mind, (whose essence is thought) and matter.

---

142. Rene. Descartes, Meditation VI: Concerning the Existence of Material Things, and the Real Distinction between Mind and Body. *Discourse on Method and Meditations on First Philosophy* 4th Edition 1998. Translated by Donald A. Cress. Hackett Publishing Company. Indianapolis Indiana.

But what relationship is there between the material and the spiritual? If David Hume's assessment that anything that we could conceive apart could logically exists apart, is anything to go by, we can rationally conclude that the notion of the un-embodied mind is conceivably and logically possible. Hence, we can conceive of mental activities (consciousness in operation- thoughts, feelings, desires) without involvement of physical brain states.

Consequently, we can conclude that the mind can exist without physical embodiment, therefore posing a defeater for the scientific theory that the brain states are where thoughts take place.

The foregoing lends support to the theistic claim, the belief that God – the Divine Mind who acts and controls things in the world is not physically embodied.

For if a conscious personally created being - man acts and operates in the world, is there any logically reason to suppose that, it is logically improbable for the uncreated Personal Divine mind to act and be in charge of affairs in the world?

What then is the relationship between the spiritual – consciousness with the material – matter? Kant believes that the material, the phenomena is separable from the spiritual, the noumena. Kant [143] differentiates between 'phenomena' as

the world as it appears to us (the observable world) in terms of how our mind perceives it, and 'noumena', the world as it is in itself (the unobservable world),which is absolutely unknown to us. But Kant conceives of noumena as a transcendental reality, something that is certainly not material but a spiritual reality.

But Kant's analysis leaves us in a dilemma of sense knowledge, the phenomena – what we can know and the noumena – the realm that requires spiritual knowledge of God, that can't be known by sense knowledge. This engenders the nature (science)

---

143. Immanuel Kant CHAPTER III Of the Ground of the Division of all Objects into Phenomena and Noumena. *THE CRITIQUE OF PURE REASON* Immanuel Kant by translated by J. M. D. Meiklejohn. Full Text internet accessed on 14.3.2013 http://philosophy.eserver.org/kant/critique-of-pure-reason.txt.

knowledge, faith knowledge divide, leading us to the prevalent problem of two systems of truth.

At this juncture, we need an integration of the truths that are inherent in both the thesis and antithesis to form a new synthesis of wholesome knowledge.

Both the thesis and the antithesis, have an intrinsic assumption of the bifurcation of reality, into scientific reality and religious reality, which by implications also filters into bifurcation of knowledge into scientific knowledge and religious knowledge. In this sense, the assumption with regard to the scientific reality/religious reality bifurcation and scientific knowledge/religious knowledge bifurcation implies that scientific reality and religious reality; and scientific knowledge and religious knowledge are mutually exclusive respectively. On a deeper level of thought however, one comes to question the validity of any arguments leading to the conclusion of the mutual exclusivity of the scientific reality/religious reality bifurcation and scientific knowledge/religious knowledge bifurcation respectively. Is there really a bifurcation or is it a false bifurcation?

What is the logical fallacy of bifurcation? It is the either -or fallacy or the false dilemma. One commits the fallacy of bifurcation when one claims that there are only two mutually exclusive options, when in actual fact, there is a third option. An example will suffice here:

"Either the church board exercises faith in this situation or they are rational about the situation."

This commits the fallacy of bifurcation since there is a third option. The church board can exercise faith and also be rational in the given situation.

The aim here is to depict how both the scientific reality/religious reality bifurcation and scientific knowledge/religious knowledge bifurcation are both a false bifurcation, since they are not in actual fact two mutually exclusive options. The reality or knowledge here, is not:

"Either scientific reality or religious reality"

And

"Either scientific knowledge or religious knowledge"

There is a third option: "There is one reality which entails both scientific and religious reality"

And

"There is absolute knowledge which entails both scientific and religious knowledge"

We are therefore, able to extract truths from both the thesis and the antithesis and consolidate the scientific reality/knowledge and religious reality/knowledge into the synthesis – the one and absolute reality / knowledge. Hence, scientific reality/knowledge and religious reality / knowledge are both each a subset of the one – absolute reality/knowledge.

If my assertion above is true, that there really is one reality which also implies that there is an objective truth, how did the division of reality and knowledge into scientific reality and religious reality, and scientific knowledge and religious knowledge occur?

As early as the fourth century, St Augustine has written extensively to address issues of relationship between nature (science) and religion. To Augustine, there is unity rather than division between nature (science) and religion. There is really one reality and Augustine assumes the unity of truth which we can learn from scripture or nature. In this sense, the two books of nature and scripture share the same divine author, God. Augustine admonishes us to be cautious in interpreting truths contained in both books to prevent conflicting interpretation thus:

"we should always observe that restraint that is proper to a devout and serious person and on an obscure question entertain no rash belief. Otherwise, if the evidence later reveals the explanation, we are likely to despise it because of our attachment to our error, even though this explanation may not be in any way opposed to the sacred writings...." [144]

---

144. Augustine, *Literal Meaning of Genesis,* Bk. II, ch. 18; 1:73.

This caution certainly was not exercised in the 17th century, by the father of the Enlightenment, Francis Bacon's interpretation of Matthew 22:29 below:

" You err, not knowing the Scriptures, nor the Power of God;"

"The other, because they minister a singular help and preservative against unbelief and error: for as our Saviour saith, You err, not knowing the Scriptures, nor the Power of God; laying before us two books or volumes to study, if we will be secured from error; first, the Scriptures, revealing the Will of God; and then the creatures expressing His Power; whereof the latter is a key unto the former: not only opening our understanding to conceive the true sense of the Scriptures, by the general notions of reason and rules of speech; but chiefly opening our belief, in drawing us into a due meditation of the omnipotency of God, which is chiefly signed and engraven upon His works." 145]

What theist Bacon did was exact opposite of Augustine's advice. He misinterpreted "the power of God," to mean the need to progress nature (science) power separately from scripture. This he did by promoting disunity of truth, and in the process created an even bigger gap between the two books of nature and scripture.

The situation has prevailed to date in the academy as defined and defended by Stephen J Gould [146] in his thesis of "non-overlapping magisteria" which is the science / religion divide.

What is general (natural) /special revelation divide? Erickson aptly describes the divide thus:

"On the one hand, general revelation is God's communication of Himself to all persons, at all times, and in all places. Special Revelation on the other hand, involves God's particular communications and manifestations which are available now only by

---

144. Augustine, *Literal Meaning of Genesis,* Bk. II, ch. 18; 1:73.

145. Francis Bacon, *Advancement of Learning* (1605), Bk I.

146. Stephen J. Gould, *Rocks Of Ages Science and Religion in the Fullness of life.* 1999 Ballantine Publishing Group p.47-68

consultation of certain sacred writings." [147]

The Middle ages scholar, Thomas Aquinas (representing the natural theology camp) and John Calvin (representing the Reformed epistemology- revealed theology camp) differ as to how God has disclosed his knowledge to man.

Natural theology is the venture to know God by reason and experience without special revelation. By contrast, revealed theology is the quest to know God by special revelation. Aquinas [148]'s view on the intellect not been affected by the Fall of man, earns him a reputation of being a pioneer who is responsible for stressing the importance of natural revelation over special revelation, thereby paving way for what Francis Schaeffer in his book 'Escape From Reason' called natural philosophy / revelation split. Schaeffer puts it thus:

"In Aquinas's view the will of man was fallen, but the intellect was not. From this incomplete view of the biblical Fall flowed all the subsequent difficulties. Man's intellect became autonomous. In one realm man was now independent, autonomous...In this view natural theology is a theology that could be pursued independently from the scriptures...he hope for unity and said that there was a correlation between natural theology and the scriptures. But the important point in what followed was a really autonomous area was set up...From the basis of this autonomous principle, philosophy also became free, and separated from revelation." [149]

Calvin [150] as well as other reformed theologians however, only accept the validity of general (natural) revelation in the context of how it is taught in scriptures. Calvin however rejects that a man

---

147. Millard J. Erickson, *Christian Theology,* 3 vols. (Grand Rapids, MI: Baker Book House, 1983), p.153.

148. Thomas Aquinas, *Summa Theologica Part 1. God's existence and nature; the creation of the world; angels; the nature of man.* From the on line Christian Classics Ethereal Library.

149. Francis Schaeffer, *Escape From Reason.* Inter-Varsity Fellowship, First Edition . 1968. p.11

150. John Calvin, *Institutes of Christian religion* Chapter 6, sections 1-4. From the On line Christian Classics Ethereal Library.

steeped in sin can come to true saving knowledge of God through general revelation. Special revelation helps man to achieve this end.

As Calvin puts it that God:

"added the light of his Word in order that he might make himself known unto salvation."[151]

In a current debate [152] on Aquinas's view that the intellect or reason was not affected by the Fall, a conclusion was reached which I think falls short of doing justice to the issue. The Fall of man affected the whole man's spirit, soul and body.

The argument here is that, the very Aquinas's stance that suggests that the Fall less probably affect the whole man ignores the noetic effects of sin. The noetic effects resulted in a twisted mind in which man has become rebellious against the will of God. It is in this sense that the noetic effects of sin negatively affect the 'sensus divinitatis' our sense of divinity or knowledge of God.

Interestingly, the cry for revival of unity of truth as Augustine conceived it is not only heard, today, in the camp of philosophers of religion, it equally echoes in the naturalists' camp. Wilson (1998), the Harvard molecular biologist's book 'Consilience The Unity Of

---

151. ibid.

152. The following question was posted by a member of the on line Academic Aquinas Forum:
"Somewhere I read that his (Aquinas's) view of the fall of man was that the intellect or reason did not fall. Does anyone know if this is an accurate portrayal of his thought?"
A response to the question goes thus:
"Aquinas believed neither that the intellect was entirely unaffected by the fall nor that the intellect fell to the level of "total depravity" (i.e., Luther and Calvin)..."
The question perfectly reflects what I consider to be a valid issue raised by Schaeffer on how Aquinas's view of the fall has consequently shaped the ensuing perception in Modern epistemology, of natural philosophy / revelation split. The response confirms my above critique of Aquinas that he ignores the noetic effects of sin on the mind and intellect.
The Aquinas list is on The Yahoo Group. The Aquinas group is intended to support thoughtful, respectful conversation about the works and ideas of St Thomas Aquinas. http://groups.yahoo.com/group/aquinas/message/50.

Knowledge' articulated the need for a synthesis of worldviews of both disciplines in the natural sciences and social sciences to form a unity of reality. Wilson's approach to try and achieve this ends fails, for the reason he gave thus:

"The main thrust of the consilience world view instead is that culture and hence the unique qualities of the human species will make complete sense only when linked in causal explanation to the natural sciences.
Biology in particular is the most proximate and hence relevant of the scientific disciplines. I know that such reductionism is not popular outside the natural Sciences." [153]

Wilson's consilience enterprise for the unity of knowledge fails. As he himself conceded in the above quote, it is a reductionist paradigm, which is a part of the antithesis in this present work. It will take the kind of synthesis attempted in this work to achieve in a true sense, the unity of knowledge that I propounded here.

However, the synthesis, in terms of the view of reality that is best suited to the delivery of a wholesome knowledge (in particular, of the Christian doxastic beliefs) is the CT conviction view of reality that promotes the influence of the universals (objective reality) over the particulars (for example, scientific endeavour). Richard Weaver [154] aptly describes the dire consequences for the objective truth of the Antithesis and its naturalistic worldview thus:

"The denial of universals carries with it the denial of everything transcending experience. The denial of everything transcending experience means—inevitably—though ways are found to hedge on this—the denial of truth. With the denial of objective truth there is no escape from the relativism of 'man the measure of all things'."

It is crucial to note that Kant's claim that 'the noumena being unobservable is unknown to us', was successfully refuted after theories were propounded in the sciences, e.g. Chemistry and

---

153. Edward O. Wilson, *Consilience*: The Unity Of Knowledge. Alfred A. Knopf, Inc., New York, in 1998
154. Richard Weaver, Ideas Have Consequences (Chicago: University of Chicago Press, 1984), 4. quoted in *"Vital Cultural Issues and Necessary Virtues"* a paper by Bruce Little Forum For Christian thought. Forumforchristianthought.com

physics that enable us to make observation into the previously unobservable world. Such a scientific feat has become the bedrock of the scientific inference to the best explanation. Theistic investigations have also benefited from employing the method of inference to the best explanation to support rational argumentation on issues ranging from the cosmological to fine tuning arguments. This is an example of how truths that are contained in the scientific antithesis have benefited the theistic thesis to contribute to synthesis agenda in this work.

The noumena as Kant conceives of it is transcendental (transcends the phenomena – the world of human experience), which is the realm of the ultimate reality of the universals. This according to Christian theism is the spirit realm from where divine mind operates and where within CT Conviction model via the deliverances of the spiritual faculty we form our Christian doxastic beliefs.

METHODOLOGICAL OUTCOME OF SYNTHESISED CT CONVICTION MODEL VIEW OF REALITY

THESIS: &   ANTITHESIS

Consist of:

THESIS	ANTITHESIS
1. Book of scripture - special revelation	1. Book of nature - natural revelation.
2. Noumena: the transcendental Objectivity.	2. Philosophical naturalism: matter, energy, space and time.
3. Deliverances of spiritual faculty.	3. Deliverances of natural sciences or five senses.

SYNTHESIS

The CT Conviction model synthesis of knowledge is predicated on the transcendental objectivity that 'God's truth is the only truth'. This presupposes that God's truth is all there is. God's truth consists of the only one reality. The only one reality incorporates the transcendental objectivity, which in turn consists of true knowledge or objective truth. Therefore God is the custodian of all knowledge or the objective reality.

The foundation of modern epistemology which Descarte's championed in his Cartesian or modern methodology of basic foundation of knowledge begins with "I," 'Cogito Ergo Sum.' 'I think therefore I am,' in which the finite knower becomes the measure of all things. This presupposes the epistemological certainty that the finite human knower can know the objective truth truly, by sense experience, howbeit, independently of transcendental objectivity. This modern or Enlightenment epistemological certainty becomes the axiom, the first principle, the assumption of philosophical naturalism, the belief that all there is, is matter, energy, space and time, as the above antithesis depicts. This modern or enlightenment quest for epistemological certainty divorced from the pre modern epistemology is the source of the bifurcation of science and religious knowledge. But as we've shown above, this naturalist reasoning commits the fallacy of bifurcation, then the argument purporting its validity is rejected and we can rationally conclude that science knowledge having originated from God's book of nature, as God's natural revelation to man, is irreducible to philosophical naturalism.

I have demonstrated in the synthesis and throughout this work that man as a finite knower, only comes to know what he knows as a created personal mind, from what the uncreated Personal Divine Mind, God exhaustively and absolutely knows. I have by rational argumentation above, demonstrated how man knows by propositional revelation that is communicated to him by the Divine mind. Hence the acquisition of knowledge by man is closely linked to revelation.
Revelation of God's absolute knowledge takes many forms as follows:

Revelation of God's absolute knowledge takes many forms as follows:

- Revelation by the natural process of the book of nature formerly known as the natural philosophy, now known as science (General revelation).

- Revelation by the inspirational book of scripture (Special revelation).

- Revelation by Divine Providence: special and general providence depicting care and government that God exercises over all he has created.

- Revelation by Reasons e.g. logical mathematical reasoning in which abstract objects such as numbers have dependent relation to God as I've discussed above.

- Revelation by dreams, visions etc.

In our postmodern world of philosophical relativism where truth has become questionable, and both the modernists (where its foundation in epistemological certainty has become, to postmodernists a fantasy, a mere myth) and post modernists (are not only relativists in their conception of truth, but has stressed relativism to the point of meaninglessness) seem to have lost the bearing of the transcendental objectivity, there is a need to promote a new normal in epistemological reality. I therefore submit that the uncreated Personal Divine mind – God is the ultimate measure of true knowledge.

Thomas Nagel in is article "What is it like to be a bat?" implies that there is something it is like to be a bat. From this analogy, I ask here, what is it like to be a Christian theist who has a perceptual experience of God? That is, what is it like to be a Christian theist who claims via the deliverances of the spiritual faculty, that he is inspired [155] by biblical revelation into having a perceptual

---

155. Romans 8:14 " For those who are led by the Spirit of God are the children of God."

experience of God? As a schema, we may ask what is it like for something to be p? What is it like for t to be p?

William James in 'The varieties of Religious Experience' explains what it is like to have a mystical experience (what is it like to be a bat?- my emphasis) thus:

"No one can make clear to another who has never had a certain feeling, in what the quality or worth of it consists. One must have musical ears to know the value of a symphony; one must have been in love one's self to understand a lover's state of mind. Lacking the heart or ear, we cannot interpret the musician or the lover justly, and are even likely to consider him weak-minded or absurd. The mystic finds that most of us accord to his experiences an equally incompetent treatment" [156]

For those who have had (Christian –my emphasis) mystical experience William James [157] said that

"mystical states seem to those who experience
them to be also states of knowledge. They are states
of insight into depths of truth unplumbed by the discursive
intellect. They are illuminations, revelations,
full of significance and importance, all inarticulate
though they remain; and as a rule they carry with
them a curious sense of authority for after-time." P367

So what is it like for a finite knower who is a Christian theist (t) to also be (p) an epistemic agent, who makes truth claims about Christianity, by operating in the deliverances of the spiritual faculty? The answer is as William James aptly puts it above, t =p, when as a finite knower, via the deliverances of the spiritual faculty, a Christian theist is endowed with insight by revelation into transcendental objective truth in forming his justified doxastic Christian beliefs, and so has knowledge.

---

156. William James, *The varieties of religious experience*: A study in human nature: being Gifford lectures on natural religion delivered at Edinburgh in 1901-1902 (1902) P.366.
157. William James, *The varieties of religious experience*. P.367.

I find compelling the following evidence given in a TV interview by a Christian paediatric surgeon who operates, the intellectual virtue of wisdom by praying for wisdom before performing most complex brain surgeries (what I describes in this dissertation as deliverances of the spiritual faculty):

"Interviewer: Dr Carson, to see a doctor and someone with so much influence and so much accomplishment to say I pray, and it's what you do boldly and all the time. So tell me what do you pray about?
Dr Carson: First of all, I pray for wisdom and guidance in everything that I do. Many people say that I'm sort of on the edge and maverick and I'm completely confident when I'm at the operating theatre. Not at all. It's just that I pray to God should I do it shouldn't I do it. Guidance in terms of how to do it. Who to consult with. All of that sort of things are incredibly important." [158]

CT CONVICTION MODEL AS AN APOLOGETIC PLOY

The practical application of the CT conviction model in our postmodern world requires a total challenge of the higher order antithesis posed by the contemporary postmodern thought, that we cannot known God because we cannot know him in an absolutist sense. I have consistently maintained so far that a personal created mind – man, is able to know the uncreated Personal Divine Mind God in virtue of man's mind being infused with consciousness by the Divine Mind, God.

As I have shown above, man's knowledge of God occurs via the production of propositional revelation by the interaction of the Divine Mind with the human mind.

Hence the Schema:

S possesses R, iff D endows S with R.

i.e. S possesses propositional revelation iff Divine Mind chooses to endow S with propositional revelation. Divine Mind- God, chooses

158. The interview of Dr Ben Carson posted on the You Tube about the *Gifted Hands Movie*. Internet accessed on 18 Jan 2013

to communicate knowledge (propositional revelation) about the natural world (science), about history and the Divine Mind has chosen to reveal it through humans (Biblical Inspiration).

The postmodern antithesis is based on the assumption, that, since we cannot know God exhaustively or omnisciently, we cannot know God at all. The Christian theist ought to counter argue that because we cannot know God exhaustively or omnisciently doesn't mean we cannot know God truly.

Knowing God omnisciently presupposes having exhaustive knowledge as God does. Of course it is impossible for a finite knower, man, to know God omnisciently (to have absolute knowledge of God) as omniscience is an incommunicable attribute of God.

"Oh, the depth of the riches of the wisdom and knowledge of God! How unsearchable his judgments, and his paths beyond tracing out!" [159]

Nevertheless, the nature/function (the intrinsic or essential qualities) of truth that is described in this work as aforementioned is a theological hypothesis that has its grounding in Christian theistic world view. Hence, we can assume a divine plan involving a finite knower – man's 'piece meal knowing of God' rather than an

'absolutist knowing of God'. In this case, our counter argument against postmodern antithesis – the requirement to have absolute knowledge before ever claiming to know God at all, is, we can know God truly, without knowing him exhaustively on this side of eternity, which is certainly more than enough to maintain an intimate relationship with God.

The phrase, finite knower - man's 'piece meal knowing of God' arises from my reading of I Corinthians 12:8, where a Christian

---

159. Romans 11:33

theist, is given "a word of knowledge" [160] by God's spirit, to know what to do in a given situation. Again this is where the Christian theist is rationally open to the CT conviction model's deliverances of spiritual faculty, and in turn is open to the process of divine revelation, to receive propositional revelation from the Divine mind – God.

As aforementioned (under closed and open systems to divine revelation) a person S who assumes a modern form of epistemology that begins with the autonomous finite self is denied access to Divine revelation on naturalistic grounds.

There is a subtle agenda behind the postmodern antithesis that we need to expose in order to logically deal with it. Its hidden agenda, is the denial of attainment of true knowledge of God. For if this is not so, why does the antithesis in contradistinction to the thesis of this work, denies, that we are in our epistemic right to hold absolute truth claims? The antithesis does so to suggest that truth is not attainable. If we buy into this antithesis we are led to subjectivity and relativity, where man once again becomes 'the measure of all things. But we've already established above in the outcome of the Hegelian dialectical triad analysis, having stripped off the falsehood associated with the antithesis to arrive at the synthesis that God is the ultimate measure of true knowledge.

Hence, continuing in our Hegelian dialectical triad analysis of reality, the former outcome, that is the synthesis – 'God

The Ultimate Measure Of true Knowledge' now becomes the new thesis.

Therefore the current postmodern antithesis becomes a false reality of knowledge as there is one reality – the new thesis, 'God The Ultimate Measure Of true Knowledge.'

So by rational argumentation the antithesis from postmodern epistemology versus the new thesis can be represented thus:

160. 1 Corinthians 12:8. This is another biblical text case of how a theistic Christian through the deliverances of spiritual faculty operates the intellectual virtues of, for example, knowledge, wisdom and understanding in addition to the biblical text case in Exodus 35:30-35.

The Argument from Postmodern Antithesis:

1. Man either possesses knowledge absolutely or there is no human knowing.

2. No man possesses knowledge absolutely.

3. Therefore no human knows anything truly.

The rational illogicality of the first premise is obvious, hence the conclusion does not follow the premises. The application of the principle of either / Or to the subject of human knowing is philosophical naïve, as it suggests that knowledge in the absolutist sense and human knowing are mutually exclusive. This assumption is also a false dilemma as it assumes that there are only two mutually exclusive possibilities, whereas there is a third alternative. The third and better alternative view in this case, is that man can know God truly without knowing God exhaustively.

The Argument from the New Thesis – 'God The Ultimate Measure Of true Knowledge'

1. There is a God who knows all things exhaustively.

2. What man knows is a fraction of the aggregate of what God knows which he discloses via natural revelation and by special revelation.

3. Therefore, man, a finite knower truly knows what God discloses to him.

Given the truth of the two premises, the conclusion logically follows. Previous philosophical arguments given above have demonstrated that the Personal Infinite God does communicate with the created personal being via propositional revelation and natural revelation.

The new normal is the synthesis - 'God, The Ultimate Measure Of true Knowledge.' This is the outcome of the Hegelian dialectical triad that I carried out above. This is now the new thesis.

This new thesis, in the light of the analysis carried out so far, assumes one reality, in which the bifurcation of nature / religion, reason /faith is disregarded and replaced with the 'unity of truth.' This 'unity of truth' accommodates features of reality from both nature / religion, reason / faith aspects of the CT Conviction model of God reality to become a new norm of 'one God reality'.

PLATO'S TRIAD VERSUS ARISTOTLE DIAD

PLATO'S TRIAD   ARISTOTLE DIAD

                       SUBJECT / OBJECT

IDEA

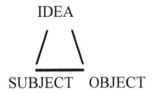

SUBJECT   OBJECT

The new norm of 'one God reality' has its root in the Plato's triad as opposed to Aristotle's diad. In the triad, the idea belongs to the realm of the supernatural for our purposes here, the transcendental, the realm of the transcendental objectivity. The idea (in the transcendental realm) plays an interpretive role, of what is real to the subject (say a human being who has an innate knowledge) about the object. (the real, the particular, say a chair)

So it is the influence from the transcendental realm that gives the subject (man) knowledge of the truth about reality of the object (we talk about having an idea, in our mind, of what the particular – the chair is.) For example the thought that one exercises, when we say (use of language) that, 'it is raining outside' corresponds to the reality that it is actually raining outside. So the relational connection in the triad is as follow:

Triad: Idea (the transcendental influence on the subject) → Subject (innate thought)

→ Word (language) → Object (reality)

The epistemic optimism 'that we can know the truth'[161] engendered by the 'realm of idea' was most graphically portrayed in the Christian theology of St Augustine in the 4th century in which he promoted as stated above the ' unity of truth' which we can learn from scripture or nature. With regards to the triad, Augustine's proposition is that 'we are created to think God's thought after him,' hence, Augustine interpreted the 'idea' as the realm of the 'Divine Mind' in its association with the 'subject' the 'human mind' which best explains the connection between the 'subject' and the 'object' – the 'chair' as the 'ideal chair' that first originated in God's mind.

This brings us to the opposing epistemological system to that of triad, that is the Aristotle's diad system that does not acknowledge the existence of (in actual fact rejects) the 'idea,' the transcendental realm as in the triad. So how does Aristotle explain, in diad, the connection, between the subject and the object and how does the subject come to have knowledge? To Aristotle, who is non metaphysical about knowledge, the knowing process simply occurs between the 'subject' (the finite knower, 'I' and the object (what is known). That is, diad is materialistic in orientation. It is bound up with subjectivity of knowing / knowledge. That is, what is truly known by the finite knower, is reducible to the senses, only empiricist about knowledge, in a world of the particulars without the influence of the universals.

Diad is the root of scepticism in epistemology, in its rejection of (the idea) the metaphysical influence on the process of knowing. The outcome as we've noted above, is, man becomes the measure of all things.

---

161. Andrew Fellows, logically deduces that Plato's Triad is epistemically consistent and promotes the 'epistemic optimism 'that we can know the truth.' Fellows contrasts this with 'epistemic pessimism' engendered by Aristotle's diad that fails to acknowledge the existence of the 'idea' the spirit or transcendental realm and its influence on how the 'subject' comes to have knowledge of the 'object' (what is real). For Fellows, Aristotle's 'diad' is the root of scepticism as we know it in epistemology today. This also leads to Fellows' distinction between the 'realists' (optimistic about the metaphysical realm) and 'normalists (sceptical about the metaphysical realm). In Andrew Fellows' lecture: *Epistemology: What is it to know?* Bethinking.Org. internet accessed on 27.3.2013

C S Lewis [162] aptly describes this epistemological tragedy as chronological snobbery, which entails the view that the achievements (theological, philosophical and scientific etc.,) of earlier time in history, are inferior to the seemingly, advanced achievements of later time in history. In my view, it is an intellectual arrogance of assumed sophistication that we can do without.

The attitude prevents us from being open to the CT Conviction model of deliverances of the spiritual faculty which is needed for gaining wholesome knowledge.

From the foregoing, we are clear as to how we get to the quest for epistemological certainty of modernism. The Enlightenment apparently, as depicted by my prior analyses, operates within the diad system of philosophical naturalism.

The dilemma however arises, as the epistemological relativism inherent in the current post modernity is also apparently, a reaction to the failure of modernity to proactively resolve issues of meaninglessness that are associated with materialism.

Undoubtedly, advancement, in science and technology, has tremendously benefited man. But how can Christian theists begin to meaningfully engage our post-modern culture? For example, we've all immensely benefited from the creation of the internet as a form of the global village, but the technology is incapacitated to correct its associated evils. This is just one simple example of how Christian ethics can help to engage and speak meaningfully to the culture in the godly use of the Web.

To get back on track to the Christian theistic (CT) Conviction model of God reality, we need to remove the clogs in the wheel of .

---

162. C S Lewis
defines this chronological snobbery as "the uncritical
acceptance of the intellectual climate of our own
age and the assumption that whatever has gone out
of date is on that count discredited." Quoted in article 'C.S. Lewis on Chronological Snobbery,' by Art Lindsley, Senior Fellow, C.S. Lewis Institute,. In Knowing & Doing. A Teaching Quarterly for Discipleship of Heart and Mind C.S. LEWIS INSTITUTE. Spring 2003. p.1. Internet accessed on 23.3.13.

the 'unity of truth' in order to kick start the biblical revelation and inspiration as a credible system of truth.

The whole of the epistemology has reached an impasse! While the triad as originally developed by Plato and modified for Christian usage by St Augustine consists essential parts that we need in order to reconnect the epistemological system back to the God reality of true knowledge, some fine tuning is required in certain areas of the triad.

In the triad, Plato dualistically separates the world of 'idea' – the spiritual realm from the material. To escape the material world, the world of 'idea,' the transcendental supernatural realm is where you take flight to. This platonic dualistic notion couldn't be farther from the ideal in the Christian theology context. From the Christian theistic theology however, we see through incarnation (integration of creator/creature, deity/humanity), Christ performing the necessary integration to connect the world of 'idea,' the spirit realm with the world of 'object,' the natural realm to bring man to wholesome knowledge of reality. It is the integration of the spiritual with the material that enhances our understanding of reality – the object. The world of idea / the world of object distinction opens the door to much of the confusion, that is brought about, for example, by Kierkegaard's development of existentialism. [163]

This distinction also informs the existential theology of thinkers including Karl Barth's existentialism, which in the main is tantamount to exclusion of God and spirituality from normal existence, in terms of his view on God / man divide. To Barth, God is 'totaliter aliter' – totally other [164].

It goes without saying that his overall existential theological system contributes to the epistemological nature / scripture divide.

Michael Polanyi however, in his book 'Personal Knowledge' insightfully argues that the object/ subject dualism commits the

163. Kierkegaard's subjective philosophy of existentialism finds expression thus:

"...the thing is to find a truth which is true for me, to find the idea for which I can live and die" Soeren Aabye Kierkegaard Journals - 1835

fallacy of bifurcation, in line with my above argument thus:

"the objective-subjective dualism is false and that all knowing of reality involves the personal commitment of the knower as a whole person" [165]

St Augustine in his Christian theological interpretation of the triad' into relationship between how the idea' (divine mind) communicates with the 'subject' (human mind), fails to address the effect of sins on the human mind.

Acknowledgement is required of the gap in the account of Plato's triad that does not take cognizance of the noetic effect of sin on the human mind. This issue has already been dealt with above with regards to getting Aquinas' account of the Fall to admit that 'sin negatively affects the 'sensus divinitatis,' our sense of divinity or knowledge of God.

Polanyi's contribution to our epistemological reconstruction of the epistemology of God reality, presupposes that we can have true knowledge of the new normal of the theistic (CT) Conviction model of God reality. To get revelation going again, unhindered from the

---

164. "Evangelical theology...had become *religionistic, anthropocentric,* and in this sense *humanistic.* What I mean to say is that an external and internal disposition and emotion of man, namely his piety – which might well be Christian piety – had become its object of study and its theme...What did it know and say of the *deity* of God? For this theology, to think about God meant to think in a scarcely veiled fashion about man, more exactly about the religious, the Christian religious man....There is no question about it: here man was made great at the cost of God – the divine God who is someone other than man, who sovereignly confronts him, who immovably and unchangeably stands over against him as the Lord, Creator, and Redeemer....The stone wall we [young theologians] first ran up against was that the theme of the Bible is the deity of *God,* more exactly God's *deity* – God's independence and particular character...God's absolutely unique existence, might, and initiative, above all, in His relation to man. Only in this manner were we able to understand the voice of the Old and New Testaments. Only with this perspective did we feel we could henceforth be theologians, and in particular, preachers – ministers of the divine Word." Barth, Karl. *Church Dogmatics.* Edinburgh, T. & T. Clark. 1977, p.39-40.

165. Michael Polanyi, *Personal Knowledge: Towards a Post-Critical Philosophy.* The University of Chicago Press .1958 P.399

triad's 'world of idea', (conceived by Augustine as) the 'divine mind,' to the 'subject' (the human mind), the remedy for sin damaged human mind needs to be accommodated within the doctrine of soteriology. [166]

This now leads us to the final gap that we need to bridge, to fully restore the epistemology of God reality. The last gap to bridge is with regard to faith / reason divide. The problem that the gap between faith and reason poses for our true knowledge of God can be resolved by once again appealing to Polanyi's concept of knowing of reality involving a holistic 'personal commitment of the knower.'

I therefore submit that there is a need to adopt a holistic approach in closing the gap between faith and reason to attain to true knowledge. I'll avoid what I reckon to be simplistic arguments on either faith is superior/inferior to reason or reason is superior/inferior to faith. This makes me an integrationist about faith/reason route to true knowledge of God.

As I have shown in all the rational argumentations in this work, both faith and reason have their places within the enterprise of knowledge. Rather than painting the picture of the two being contradictory, I'm interested in articulating here, that they are in actual fact, complementary. Hence the holistic approach that I prefer is faith / reason integrationist approach that is open to the deliverances of the spiritual faculty. The following is the reason for this.

As admitted above, we've got to make allowance for necessary repairs to be carried out on the rational faculty – the mind, which was damaged by the noetic effects of sin.

This requires the infusing of the damaged human mind with divine revelation in order for renewal of man's mind to be achieved. The only access to divine

---

166. The doctrine of soteriology is the Christian doctrine of salvation. The means by which the soul of man is saved from sin and its eternal consequences.

revelation is faith. There is a consensus in the academy, that there are two approaches to faith. The epistemological and soteriological approaches. The epistemological approach is represented by Aquinas's work involving the role of reason in attaining knowledge via natural revelation. The soteriological approach is reflected in the works of reformers, including John Calvin and Martin Luther.

Soteriology being the doctrine of salvation, the means by which the noetic effects of sin and its negative effects on the mind is dealt with, in order for man to become renewed and ready to receive fresh revelation from God.

Once the mind is renewed via the saving faith, man's mind is ready for free, unhindered flow of revelation from the divine mind, via the CT Conviction model of deliverances of the spiritual faculty. The Christian theist is therefore justified in holding Christian doxastic beliefs.

LIMERICK CITY AND COUNTY LIBRARY

SUMMARY AND CONCLUSION

A multifaceted problem drives my intention, to argue, in Part 11 of this book, for the thesis, that – 'the deliverances of the spiritual faculty;' form our justified Christian doxastic beliefs, which also as a cognitive faculty, informs the process of acquiring knowledge by the use of the spiritual sense within the CT Conviction Model, that I developed. To paint with a broad brush, the issues involved, are as categorised below:

Christian conviction: As tersely noted in chapter 13, the place for the importance of conviction for which Christian doxastic beliefs are held, have been almost completely eroded, by the nebulous relativist conception of truth in our post-modern culture.

Private / Public domains: Another important phase of the problem is how the church has compromised to allow the truth that we genuinely have in divine revelation, to be driven into the private domain of our lives, when God originally intends that this truth about reality be held and shared in the public domain. For example, the church in debates with the 21st Century sophisticated, tough-minded non Christians, has often bought into the subtle compromise that allows non Christians to 'set the agenda' as to what belongs to the 'private' or the 'public' domains of our lives. For example, we hear non Christians say:

' you can hold on to your Christian beliefs as long as you don't bother me about those beliefs in the public domain.'

Trivialising the spiritual: The fundamental, and the most important phase of the problem is the triviality with which 'spiritual' concepts are held, in the academy with regards to discourse on rationality for holding Christian beliefs based on biblical revelation and inspiration. The spiritual, the metaphysical or the transcendental issues are made to sound weird, unacceptable, irrational, not worth engaging in, rationally 'since you cannot provide empirical evidence' so thinks the empiricist / naturalist.

My research however, indicates that from around 428 BC, Plato in his triad, (see chapter 13), introduces the philosophical notion of the 'idea' or 'the world of idea' which is the transcendental or the spirit realm. The church father Origen also implies what I call the 'deliverances of the spiritual faculty in contradistinction to what he calls 'a natural faculty' (see chapter 12, footnote 125).

There seems to be more to the 'spiritual' than meets the eye. I therefore submit, that there is still a lot yet, to be discovered in this area, in order to be better informed about the Christian doxastic beliefs- forming potential of the deliverances of the spiritual faculty' of the CT Conviction model.

Therefore, in Chapter 7, I critique, in order to identify issues for further analysis in the subsequent chapters and so add my contribution in filling the gap, as I see it that exists with the prudential and basicality of belief forming produced by Pascal, James and Plantinga and the belief forming 'deliverances of the spiritual faculty' within my CT Conviction model thesis.

In Chapter 8, my CT Conviction model of doxastic justification is geared towards differentiating the propositional justification from dosaxtic justification, thereby positing the importance of doxastic justification, in being epistemically justified in holding a belief.

In chapter 9 by employing Alston's concept of epistemic desiderata, that allows beliefs in general, but I find his pluralistic approach, in particular, useful for Christian doxastic beliefs to be evaluated from variety of the epistemic points of view. This particularly assists me to further develop the CT Conviction model as a truth conducive epistemic desideratum with a truth goal of maximal truth and minimal falsehood for beliefs. For example, as analysed in chapter 12, under my CT conviction model of the theory of epistemic justification, the probability of producing justified Christian true beliefs (jcb) in a 'large body of beliefs,' given that they are based on biblical injunctions as adequate grounds (g) is very high thus:

S's belief that $p \Rightarrow P(jcb/g) > 0.95$.

In chapters 10, 11, and 13 respectively, I produce rational argumentation to substantiate the correlation between the Divine Mind, God and the human mind, that makes divine communication feasible. Also by rational argumentation, I hypothesize how the infusing of the essence of the Divine Consciousness into human consciousness is possibly, the source of the human consciousness.

The various analyses and philosophical arguments that I produce in the book cumulatively lead me to postulate in chapter 13, a CT Conviction model thesis, view of reality, in which I employ the methodological Hegelian dialectical traid of theistic thesis, the naturalist antithesis, which results in the outcome, that is,
the synthesis – 'God The Ultimate Measure Of true Knowledge'

I envision the outcome becoming an apologetic ploy for engaging the culture more meaningfully, in understanding the strategic importance of Christian conviction for our Christian doxastic beliefs that have adequate grounds in biblical inspiration and revelation.

If adopted in the academy, my theory of epistemic justification of Christian doxastic beliefs that are formed by the 'deliverances of the spiritual faculty' within the CT Conviction model, will serve as part of a necessary impetus for a paradigm shift from the epistemology of two systems of truth to the only one reality, 'God The Ultimate Measure Of true Knowledge.'

I essentially argue in Part 11, that there is such a thing on the Christian theistic conception of truth, which in my phraseology is 'the deliverances of the spiritual faculty' that has a higher explanatory power of reality from the Christian worldview.

CONCLUDING THOUGHT:

To be current and coherent therefore, the 'intellectual community' (a construct) consisting of wider 'epistemic communities' that I have suggested in this book, ought to be a dynamic community. So that, in our acquisition and implementation of knowledge of any aspects of reality, the scale always, tips more in the direction of rationality based on aggregate of sources of knowledge rather than just empirical objectivity.

This dynamic way of thinking, is pivotal to the purpose of my main thesis of 'unity of knowledge', that there is no justification for the notion of absolute objectivity of scientific truth to the nullification of say, the theological truth. Hence the need for the unity of knowledge within a whole system approach to the coherence theory of truth.

APPENDIX

AN HISTORICAL ANALYSIS OF THE TRANSITION FROM THE GOD CENTRED REALITY TO POST MODERNITY

The theological world view or the God-centred view of reality predominated our universal perception of truth in pre-modern era. There was a paradigm shift from pre-modern God centred reality to modern thought, that is, the enlightenment naturalism in the 17th century, the period which included the age of reason in the 18th Century. Yet another paradigm shift occurred from modern thought to the contemporary post-modern thought namely, pragmatism and existentialism.

Philosophically, theistic realism[i] described the pre 17th century, pre-modern God centred reality. In the literature, the correspondence theory of truth prevailed during this era up to the 19th century. In pre modern time, when a thought or a statement perfectly described reality, such a thought or statement was true. There were fixed parameters around certain things that assigned such things truth value. That is, such things were universally true, for everyone everywhere, regardless of whether or not anyone believed it or not. Acceptance of the supernatural and of course mythology was common place in the pre modern world. Hence, truth was a derivative of revelation from the Holy Scripture, dictates of tradition and directives of authoritative leaders.

It was little wonder then, that the advocates of the modern thought found the hierarchical and authoritative structure of the pre modern thought repulsive. It was repulsive to the modern man because it presupposed the notion of absolute objective truth as 'given', given by God or the gods. I think that the evasive lumping of pagan tradition including the myth of the age, and the God centred Christian tradition of the same era as constituting truth, reality or what was real, left more to be desired.

Incoherence that resulted from presupposed truth from pagan

---

[i] Theistic realism is a philosophy based on the idea that God is real, acts in the universe, and is knowable through the senses and reason. "http://creationwiki.org/Theistic_realism"Category:Philosophy. Internet; accessed 1 Jan 2011.

mythology and truth from revelation from God of Abraham, Isaac and Jacob was apparent to the rational modern man of the early 17th century. The pre modern man never really specifically answered the question, 'who really rules over creation?' If any answer was given to this question, it would be, God or the gods? The ambiguity that this answer presupposed, convinced the proponents of modernism that the notion of absolute truth that pre modernism espoused was nonsensical and couldn't be further from the truth. So, to the modern man of the modern era of the enlightenment naturalism and the age of reason in the 18th century, rationalism and scientific knowledge were supreme.

Lest we forget the dark ages (middle ages). The conversion of Emperor Constantine in the 4th century to Christianity led to Christianity becoming the official State religion of the Roman Empire under Constantine. At the collapsed of the Western Roman Empire, with its attendant problems of chaotic administrative, economic and legal disorder, the Church took the initiative for restoring order.

The ungodly practices involving decadence and debauchery of the Church of Rome however, in the 14th century led to revolt against the church's stance that denied ordinary Christians access to the bible. Up till then, the Bible was only available in Latin and opened only to exclusive clubs of Roman Catholic priests. John Wycliffe who first translated the Bible into English was persecuted as a heretic by removal from his position as an Oxford Scholar.

There was light at the end of the tunnel though. It was reformation led by Martin Luther in the 16th century that eventually nailed the coffin of the church's corruption and decadence. An example of such unbiblical doctrine of the Church of Rome, is that of granting indulgences to atone for sins. For instance, going on a crusade to the holy land would get you forgiveness for sins you ever committed.

Purchase of indulgences at your death bed would give you a direct transport to heaven, thereby bypassing purgatory.

Luther, an Augustinian monk, repulsed by the ungodly Vatican order, developed the doctrine of grace against the Church of Rome's doctrine of selling indulgences for forgiveness of sins. This later became the protestant theology, that salvation can only be received as a gift from God not as indulgence that the Church sells for economic gain. The scripture that inflamed Luther's soul as he agonized over the Church's corruption and manipulation with regard to the doctrine of indulgence was first cited in the prophecy of Habakkuk 2:4

" But the just shall live by his faith."

Then the scripture appeared thrice in the New Testament: Romans1:17, Galatians 3:11 and Hebrew 10:38 consecutively. Luther in a revolt to the Church of Rome posted his famous "Ninety-Five Theses" on the door of All Saints Church in Wittenberg on 31 October 1517, which resulted in his excommunication from the church. Thanks to the advent of Gutenberg printing press, Luther's protest was widely circulated. Putting the press to good use, Luther produced a translation of the Bible into German thus given ordinary people access to the truth of the Bible. Before then the church had persecuted people who had attempted to interpret the Bible to other languages other than Latin which only Catholic priests were allowed access. The knowledge of the Bible spread amongst members of the general public, especially in England where translations of the bible into English by both William Tyndale and John Wycliffe had been combined to form the King James Bible. This breakthrough exposed the corruption in the church but resulted in Renaissance with its characteristic humanistic agenda. A departure from God centred perspective to a humanistic world view.

It was zeal without knowledge. The Church of Rome's opposition to the progress of science 'in the case of persecution of Galileo for his heliocentric planetary system of sun centred universe at the beginning of the 17th century, which was in actual fact proven true, was used as an example of the need to abandon the pre modern thought for a human centred weltanchaaung. The church's antagonism, of course was a case of blind commitment to a man made theological doctrine. It can be affirmed that the church as God intended, is the pillar of truth, and that authentic Christian theistic world view does not condone falsehood in any form or shape.

Hence, with the rise of humanistic movement, came the civil leadership that ripped the Church of Rome its governmental authority. The Church of Rome was to be blamed for its predicament for departing from the spirit of justice and morality that Christianity as clearly depicted in the Bible enjoins.

It was the reformers who began to restore dignity to the moral fibre of the society at large by promoting the reading and study of the entire Bible amongst the general public as Barbara Tuchman [ii] put it:

"With the translation of the Bible into English and its adaptation as the highest authority for an autonomous English Church, the history, traditions and moral code of the Hebrew nation became for a period of three centuries the most powerful single influence on that culture."

It must be the truth, nothing but the whole truth. The history of the 17th century as the age of the enlightenment, extending into the eighteen century, the age of reason, as is often depicted in the literature is a lopsided one, since it fails to account for the Bible's influence on the political and social landscape of Europe at the time. Starting from England, the Puritan revolution was instrumental in purging the Church of England of the spiritual failings of the Roman Catholic Church, by promoting a bible based culture, incorporating total adherence to the just practices of the Bible. The Puritan Revolution was so successful that it impacted the political life of the nation. The Puritan sought to implement the aim of the reformation, that every man has the right to appeal to the law of God above the human authority, in the main, the power of the Monarch; so much so that the English Parliament was able to bring the Monarch to book over corruption.

The intent of the Puritans was to purify the Church of England of its Catholic roots. To the Puritans, the Church of England was extremely corrupt and still too Catholic, an indication of the influence of the Church of Rome. To this end, they advocated for a total reformed protestantism without any Catholic influence.

The puritans argued that allegiance was due only to the Almighty God and not to any human, Monarch, or any religious figure. The

---

ii. Tuchman Barbara, The Bible and the sword, New York University Press, 1956, p.80

Puritans' obsession for advocating theocracy – absolute authority of God's law above the authority of the monarch in England, led to the in which King Charles 1 of England was the contender.

At stake in the Eight year long Civil war was the question: Should England be governed by the democratic Parliament consisting mostly of divine justice conscious members or the autocratic power drunk monarch? The masses represented by the Parliament won. The ruling monarch Charles 1 was tried and executed and Oliver Cromwell became in 1653, the head of state as the Lord Protector. The monarch again gained power from the Parliament after the death of Oliver Cromwell in 1658. This ended the Puritan domination of England. The Puritan for religious reasons - they intended to build a new society based on biblical laws and teachings, left England in search of a colony to practice religious freedom. They landed at what is now called Plymouth, Massachusetts USA.

History depicts that the Puritan Revolution influenced other revolutions in Europe, for example, the French Revolution, and the Russian Revolution. Indeed the American Revolution was an offshoot of the original purpose behind the English or Puritan Revolution.

The puritans in their religious zeal promoted within the society, adherence to morality and a civil society in line with bible injunctions. The impact on the general public of its exposure to reading the Bible was an improvement in the literacy level of the populace. Spiro (2002:240) put it thus:

"As a result of this outlook, by the end of the seventeenth century and certainly by the beginning of the eighteenth century, about 40 percent of the adult male population of Protestant Europe could read. To us today, 40 percent may seem low, but compared to the abysmal literacy rates of Greco-Roman times or to the Dark Ages when Catholic clergy kept books under lock and key, 40 percent seems like a tremendous significant leap forward."

The truth that is often left out of the history of the Enlightenment is that the springboard for the Enlightenment was the revolt of the English Protestants against tyrannical monarchy. This revolt by the Protestants, in the main the Bible believing Puritans, helped to overthrow the tyrannical Catholic king James 11 who was replaced by Protestant monarchs, Queen Mary 11 and her husband King Williams. The Parliament at this stage ensured that the executive power resided with the Parliament resulting in the Monarch becoming only a figurehead. This revolt led to the "Glorious Revolution" which resulted in the English government's promulgation of a Bill of Rights, which consequently resulted in a greater level of personal freedoms for the general populace. The Enlightenment thinkers in all walks of life grabbed this opportunity to promote novelty in scientific, philosophical, political, social and economic theories. The Enlightenment thinkers and in turn the enlightened populace became poised for democratic society, having freedom to take lead in the scientific, social economic and political arenas of the society.

I submit therefore, that the springboard for our Western Enlightenment, is the biblical truth that truly liberates. Hence,

" ----you shall know the truth and the truth shall set you free." [iii]

---

iii. John 8:32 NIV.

BIBLIOGRAPHY

Achebe, Chinua. *Things Fall Apart*. William Heinemann Ltd UK 1958.

Alston. William P, *Beyond Justification: Dimensions of Epistemic Evaluation*, Cornell University Press, Ithaca and London. 2005

Alston. William P, *Divine Mystery and Our Knowledge of God*. In the three lectures given by Alston (read by Nicholas Wolterstorff) at Yale Divinity School Convocation 2005 uploaded by Yale Divinity School www.youtube.com/watch?v=WOYib0Zm9W8 *internet accessed on 10.2.2013.Lecture* I: The Divine Mystery Thesis. Lecture II: Why We Should Take Divine Mystery Seriously, Lecture III: The Need For True Statements About God.

Alston, William P. *Perceiving God: The Epistemology of Religious Experience*. Cornell University Press. 1993.

Aquinas, Thomas. *Summa Theologica Part 1. God's existence and nature; the creation of the world; angels; the nature of man*. From the on line Christian Classics Ethereal Library.

Aquinas, Thomas. *Summa Theologica I, Q. 3, A. 3 "On the Simplicity of God"*. Many editions. Quoted in an article "Divine Simplicity" in Wikipedia on line Encyclopedia. Internet accessed on 6 Feb 20133.

Anselm (1033-1109): *Proslogium*. CHAPTER XV – "He is greater than can be conceived."Fordham University Of New York.

Augustine, *Literal Meaning of Genesis*, Bk. II, ch. 18; 1:73.

Augustine, De diversis quaestionibus octoginta tribus, 46.2. trans. David L. osher (Washington D. C.: The Catholic University of America Press), 80-81.

Bacon, Francis, *Advancement of Learning* (1605), Bk I.

Barth, Karl. *Church Dogmatics*. Edinburgh, T. & T. Clark. 1977.

Barnard, Robert. *"Review of "Beyond Justification: Dimensions of Epistemic Evaluation","* Essays in Philosophy: Vol. 8: Iss. 2, Essays in Philosophy is a biannual journal published by Pacific University Library 2007 | http://commons.pacificu.edu/eip/

Becker. K, *"Reliabilism"* a peer review of Goldman's process Reliabilism. Internet Encyclopedia of Philosophy 2009 –a peer reviewed academic resource. www.iep.utm.edu/reliabil.

Bengtsson, David. *'The Nature Of Explanation In A Theory Of Consciousness*, p.2 Kungshuset, Lundagård 222 22 Lund. David.Bengtsson@fil.lu.se,

Bonjour, Laurence. *In Defense of Pure Reason*, [New York: Cambridge University Press, 1998

Calvin, John, *Institutes of Christian religion* Chapter 6, sections 1-4. From the On line Christian Classics Ethereal Library.

Collin, Francis. *'The Language Of God. A Scientist Presents Evidence for Belief.'* Pocket Books, Simon & Schuster UK Ltd. 2007.

Conn, Christopher, *"Chisholm, Internalism, and Knowing That One Knows."* American Philosophical Quarterly, Vol. 38, No. 4 (Oct., 2001), p. 333

Chisholm, Roderick. The Problem of the Criterion Publisher Marquette University Press Milwaukee.1973.

Chisholm, Roderick. Theory of knowledge (Englewood Cliffs, N.J.: Prentice Hall).1989.

Clifford, W. K. *"The Ethics of Belief." Lectures and Essays.* London: Macmillan, 1879.

Corey, Michael A. *Supernatural Agency and the Modern Scientific Method,* a paper presented at the Christian Scholarship: Knowledge, Reality, and Method Conference, held on October 9-11th (1997) at the University of Colorado at Boulder. Available from Internet; access www.leaderu.com/aip/docs/corey.html. Internet; accessed 6 Jan, 2010.

Dawkins, Richard. *The Blind Watchmaker.* New York: W. W. Norton & Company, Inc. 2006.

Dennett. Daniel, 1993. Consciousness Explained Penguin Books Ltd.

Descartes, R. *Discourse on Method and The Meditations On First Philosophy* 4th Edition 1998. Translated by Donald A. Cress. Hackett Publishing Company. Indianapolis Indiana.

Dickson, John *'Why Historians Take The Gospel Seriously',* a presentation at Saddleback Church Lake Forrest California 2011 by Dr Dickson of the Department of Ancient History, Macquarie University Sydney, Australia.

Erickson, Millard J. *Christian Theology,* 3 vols. (Grand Rapids, MI: Baker Book House, 1983).

Fellows, Andrew. ' lecture: *Epistemology: What is it to know?* Bethinking.Org. Internet accessed on 27.3.2013.

Foster, John. *"Regularities, Laws of nature and the Existence of God".* Proceedings of the Aristotelian Society, New Series, Vol. 101, (2001), pp. 145-161

Flew, Anthony .*There Is A God: How the World's Most Notorious theist Changed His Mind.* Goldman, Alvin I. "Epistemic Folkways and Scientific Epistemology." In Liaisons: Philosophy Meets the Cognitive and Social Sciences. Cambridge, Mass.: The MIT Press, 1992.

Frank, Jackson. *"Epiphenomenal Qualia." The* Philosophical Quarterly, Vol. 32, No. 127. (Apr., 1982), pp. 127-136.

Goldman, Alvin I. 1992. *"Epistemic Folkways and Scientific Epistemology."* In Liaisons: Philosophy Meets the Cognitive and Social Sciences. Cambridge, Mass.: The MIT Press, 1992.

GOLDMAN, Alvin I. *Naturalistic Epistemology and Reliabilism.* Midwest Studies In Philosophy, 1994: 301–320.

Goldman, Alvin I. *"What Is Justified Belief?"* in G. Pappas, ed. Justification and Knowledge (Dordrecht: D. Reidel),1979: 1-23.

Greco, John. *Internalism And Epistemically Responsible Belief.* Synthese 85, 245-277 1990, 1990 Kluwer Academic Publishers. Printed in Netherlands.

Greco, John. *Virtue Epistemology* in A Companion to Epistemology Second Edition edited by JONATHAN DANCY,ERNEST SOSA, and MATTHIAS STEUP A John Wiley & Sons, Ltd., Publication 2010. P.75

Gould, Stephen J. *Rocks Of Ages – Science And Religion In The Fullness Of Life*. Published by Jonathan Cape 2001.

Hartman, Robert S. *The Knowledge of Good: Critique of Axiological Reason* (Value Inquiry Book) 2002 Chapter 10: Synthetic Value Measurement and Prediction p.325.

Hume, David. *Dialogues Concerning Natural Religion*, edited with an introduction by Norman Kemp Smith, (New York: Social Sciences Publishers, 1948.

Hume, David. *An Enquiry Concerning Human Understanding*. 2nd Ed, Hackett Publishing Company, Inc, Indianapolis, Indiana, 46244-0937. 1993.

Hawking Stephen, Leonard, Mlodinow. The Grand Design New Answers To The Ultimate Question Of Life, published by Bantam Books in 2010

James, William. *The Will to Believe.* New York: Longmans, Green & Co., 1897.

James, William. *The varieties of religious experience*: A study in human nature: being Gifford lectures on natural religion delivered at Edinburgh in 1901-1902 (1902) P.366.

Kant, I. *Critique of Pure Reason,* 1787, second edition, translated by N. Kemp-Smith, London: Macmillan, 1933. 1.

Kemp, Kenneth W. *"Scientific Method and Appeal to Supernatural Agency"*: A Christian Case for Modest Methodological Naturalism. Available from http://w"ww.stthomas.edu/cathstudies/logos/archives/volumes/3-2/kemp.pdf. Internet; accessed Feb 14, 2010.

Kierkegaard, Soeren Aabye. *"Soeren Aabye Kierkegaard"* Journals – 1835.

Kuhn, Thomas S. *The Structure of Scientific Revolutions.* 2d ed. Chicago: University of Chicago Press 1970.

Lamont, John. *Divine Faith,* Ashgate Publishing Limited England 2004.Leite. Adam,

Leite, Adam. '*What the Basing Relation can Teach Us About the Theory of Justification*' by, Indiana University, Bloomington www.indiana.edu/~episteme/Abstracts/JustifyingAbstract.pdf. Internet accessed on 14 November 2012.

Lindsley, Art. *"C.S. Lewis on Chronological Snobbery,"* Lindsley, Senior Fellow, C.S. Lewis Institute,. In Knowing & Doing. *A Teaching Quarterly for Discipleship of Heart and Mind* C.S. LEWIS INSTITUTE. Spring 2003.

Medawar, Peter *'The limits of Science'* (Oxford University Press (1987)

Munitz, Milton K. *Cosmic Understanding: Philosophy and Science of the Universe.* Princeton University Press, 1990.

Nagel, Thomas. *"What is it like to be a bat?"* From The PhilosophicalReviewLXXXIII,4(October1974):43550]http://organizations.utep.edu/portals/1475/nagel_bat.pdf

Origen 1953:*Contra Celsum,* VI, 10, p. 324.

Pascal, Blaise. 1910. *Pascal's Pensées,* translated by W. F. Trotter.

Plantinga, *Alvin. "An Evolutionary Argument Against Naturalism"* by Prof. Alvin Plantinga. The outline of the lecture Prof. Plantinga gave at BIOLA University. Calvin Collegewww.calvin.edu/.../plantinga.../an_evolutionary_argument_again st_ ... Internet accessed on 13 Jan 2013.

Plantinga, Alvin (2000), *Warranted Christian Belief*, Oxford: Oxford University Press.

Polanyi, Michael. '*Personal Knowledge: Towards a Post-critical Philosophy.*' 1958, Reprinted 1998, 2002 Routledge, 11 New Fetter Lane, London EC4P 4EE.

Polkinghorne, John. Serious Talk:Science and Religion in Dialogue. (1995)

Putnam, Hilary. *Reason, Truth And History*. Cambridge University Press, 1981 p.5. The Edinburgh Building, Cambridge CB2 2RU, UK http: //www.cup.cam.ac.uk. Internet accessed 29 Oct 2011.

Reid, Thomas. *Essays on the Intellectual Powers of Man,* reprinted in Thomas Reid, The Works of Thomas Reid, William Hamilton, ed., 5th Ed. (Edinburgh: Maclachlan and Stewart, 1958), VI, v, 447.

Ruse, Michael. *Science and Spirituality – Making room for faith in the age of science*, Cambridge University Press; 1 edition (March 8, 2010)

Savage, C Wade *"The Paradox of the Stone."* In *The Philosophical Review*, Vol. 76, No. 1. (Jan., 1967), pp. 74-79

Schaeffer, Francis. , *Escape From Reason.* Inter-Varsity Fellowship, First Edition . 1968.

Schaeffer, Francis. *He is there and he is not silent,*. Tyndale House Publishers, Wheaton Illinois. 1972.

Schwartz, Jeffrey M, Henry P. Stapp, Mario Beauregard. QUANTUM PHYSICS IN NEUROSCIENCE AND PSYCHOLOGY A NEUROPHYSICAL MODEL OF MIND/BRAIN INTERACTION. Section 5.2. p. 31

Stephen, Covey R. The 7 Habits of Highly Effective People, Simon & Schuster UK Ltd 1989, 2004 p.65

Swinburne, Richard."Review of *Warranted Christian Belief* by Alvin Plantinga", *Religious Studies*, (2001), 37: 203–214.

Swinburne, Richard. The Existence of God (NY: Clarendon) 1991.

Swinburne, Richard. *Epistemic Justification by Richard Swinburne* Oxford University Press, 2001.

The Apostle Creed. "English translation of the Apostles' Creed in the Catechism of the Catholic Church". Va. 1997-03-25. http://www.va/archive/catechism/p1s1c3a2.htm#credo. Retrieved 2011-05-19. Quoted in articled titled Apostle Creed in Wikipedia, the online Encyclopedia. Internet accessed on 7.2.2013.

The Holy Bible, New King James Version, Thomas Nelson, Inc. 1982.

The Holy Bible, New International Version, International Bible Society 1973.

Turri, John. "*On the relationship between propositional and doxastic justification.*" Philosophy and Phenomenological Research, Volume 80, Issue 2, pages 312–326, March 2010.

Weaver, Richard. Ideas Have Consequences (Chicago: University of Chicago Press, 1984

Wilson, Edward O. *Consilience*: The Unity Of Knowledge. Alfred A. Knopf, Inc., New York, in 1998.

Zagzebski, Linda. *Virtues of the Mind:* An Inquiry into the Nature of Virtue and the Ethical Foundations of Knowledge. Cambridge: Cambridge University Press. 1996.

INDEX

This form of indexing will ensure that the reader has a quick overview of the entire 'Unity Of Knowledge' thesis that this book espouses. It also provides space for the reader's notes on useful terms of the thesis.

A

J

Lightning Source UK Ltd.
Milton Keynes UK
UKHW01f2025310818
328139UK00001B/88/P

9 781526 202253